Borderlir

more murder cases from the Scottish Borders

Norrie McLeish

ALBA PUBLISHING

Borderline Cases
Norrie McLeish
ISBN 1-873-708-11-4

Published by Alba Publishing
20 Dounehill
Jedburgh
TD8 6LJ

Printed by Kelso Graphics

Other Books by Norrie McLeish

Ancestral Voices - The Story of the McLeish Name
Death in the Borders - 19th century border murder cases
The Haunted Borders

As Editor
Glimpses into the Past in Lammermuir (First edition)
Glimpses into the Past in Lammermuir (Second Edition)
Tales of a Grenadier
Jethart Worthies

Work in Progress
Broken Promises 19th century breach of promise cases

This book is dedicated to my
four sons, Jeb, David, Martyn and Mark.
They have all turned out smarter than
their Dad - or so they keep telling me.

Contents

Illustrations

My thanks to Scottish Borders Archives at St Marys Mill in Selkirk for their permission to use the pictures on pp 46,54 and 86.
Thanks also to the Old Gala Club for their permission to use the picture on p74.

Acknowledgements

First my thanks to the many local people who helped me track down the locations mentioned in the book. It is surprising how many people come up to you when you are standing looking around with a note-book in your hand. After about half an hour you have a very different perspective on the place around you. So to all those people who spoke to me and provided me with invaluable snippets of information my grateful thanks.

I also have to acknowledge the help of those people who actually live in the the place where a murder took place. Fortunately all of them knew something about it so I wasn't the bearer of unwelcome news. I never quite managed to get used to knocking on a door and saying; "Excuse me but did you know there was a murder in your house!"

As ever my grateful thanks to the staff at the Scottish Records Office and the Scottish National Library in Edinburgh. Particular thanks to the staff at the Scottish Borders Archives at St Mary's Mill in Selkirk who were as cheerful and as professional as ever in providing me with fascinating material from their vast repository of local material. Thanks to to the staff of Kelso Library and my local one in Jedburgh.

Roy Ledsham in Jedburgh and Hugh Mackay of Hawick as well as my wife Isobel were invaluable in checking over the text for spelling and stylistic errors. Any errors of fact, of which I trust there are few, are mine and mine alone.

Introduction

After my book, 'Death in the Borders', came out, a number of people said it seemed that murders were quite commonplace in the Borders last century. It is the opposite that is true. A glance through the Criminal Precognition records (AD14 series) in the Scottish Record Office quickly establishes that murders in the Borders in the 19th century were few and far between. A similar undertaking using the records of Edinburgh or Glasgow would run to many volumes. It is because murder was such an extremely unusual crime that it excited so much interest among Border people of the time. I was struck by the fact that when a murder trial was held in Jedburgh Circuit Court the public galleries were always packed with spectators at once fascinated and appalled. Only a minority of murder trials in Glasgow or Edinburgh attracted such numbers. It is important therefore to state at the outset that murder was not an activity indulged in by the majority of Borderers.

Other people were curious to know why I was so interested in murders. Some, on hearing my accent, assumed that it was down to my Glasgow upbringing. Now. I must confess that I have known, fairly well, two convicted murderers. This, I hasten to add, is a pretty uncommon occurrence - even for a Glaswegian. This experience certainly made me reflect on the nature of murderers for although both were rightly convicted, nothing in their early lives suggested to me that they would turn into murderers. Indeed, if I had been told that two people I knew would turn out to be murderers these two would have been well down the list. It is only after the event, when we look back and try and reshape our memories that we claim that certain events and incidents should have shown us that they were going to turn out to be murderers. But of course hindsight makes geniuses of us all. The truth is that given certain circumstances and pressures all of us are capable of killing. It is part of the human condition.

The very word 'murder' is itself ambiguous. When I was researching 'Death in the Borders' it had the working title of "Border Murders' Now after reading several Criminal Precognitions I was in no doubt that several men were guilty of murdering their wives, the evidence seemed to me to be overwhelming. But 19th century all-male juries thought otherwise, particularly if it could be shown that the wife had some kind of perceived flaw in her character. They invariably accepted his claim that it was an accident and a 'not guilty' or 'not proven' verdict was given. Technically no murder had been committed.so I could not really call the book 'Border Murders.' There is a clear legal distinction between the crime of 'murder' and that of 'culpable homicide.' It is one of the arguments against the reintroduction of capital punishment that juries were very reluctant to find a man guilty when they knew that he would be executed. Many 'murder' charges were reduced to the lesser charge of 'culpable homicide.' Although often it was a very fine legal distinction..

In the 19th century when life was harsh and there were no safety nets for the poor, death was a frequent visitor. Police presence was sparse, particularly in rural areas and forensic medicine was in its infancy. Murder, I suspect, was much more frequent than the official records show. How many husbands, I wonder, passed away from 'gastric problems'? The importance of personal hygiene was not widely appreciated, it was the wives who did the cooking and knowledge of the toxic properties of plants was better known than it is now. So ,while it has often been remarked that there were very few female murderers, it could be that they were cleverer in the planning and execution of the deed as well as the covering-up. I would hasten to add that there is absolutely no evidence to back up this particular point of view. The first half of the 19th century saw a large number of young women brought to trial for murdering their newly born child. The frequency of this crime of 'infanticide' reduced as society became a bit less intolerant of unmarried girls who became pregnant.

In this book I have ventured a bit further in time and have even departed from the strict boundaries of the Scottish Borders on two occasions. While murder was not uncommon in the 16th century Borderland, the killing of Anthony de la Bastie was a significant event in Scottish history and illustrates the savage tribal nature of Border society of the time. Similarly, I have always found the case of John Kello, the minister of Spott to be a fascinating one. As Spott lies on the northern slopes of the Lammermuir hills, I felt I could justify its inclusion. It is a strange, dramatic tale and it must have been a severe embarrassment to John Knox's newly reformed church. But their '16th century spin-doctors' were quick to turn it to their advantage; this however presupposed the unfortunate John Kello's guilt. Nowadays we are more aware of the strange workings of the human sub-conscious and of the dark workings of the human mind. John Kello could have been a man torn apart by guilt and determined that he would punish himself.

I go back to the 18th century for two other cases. The murder of Lady Billie is well-known in the eastern Borders. The strange affair at Greystonelees farm less so. In both these cases I had to rely on newspaper reports and articles as the legal records had been lost. By doing so I hope that I have managed to cast a little light on how difficult it was for justice to be obtained for those with little or no influence.

Strangely enough, Hawick is the only place in the Borders in the 19th century where a man was found guilty of murdering his wife. Some unkind folk have actually suggested that it was not the weight of evidence that decided his fate , but the fact that the husband originally came from Ayr and that his wife was Hawick born. Setting that aside, it is ironic that the only instance of a husband being executed for the murder of his wife should be one where his guilt is in some doubt. The fact that this drama was played against the background of the presence of French prisoners of war who must have brought some 'glamourie' to Hawick makes it all the more fascinating.

The 'culture of drink' which held sway in the Borders found its victims in Coldstream, St Boswells and Galashiels long before the murders in these places were committed. Alcohol is still the most dangerous drug in society but its effects were unrestrained and widespread in Victorian Scotland. Perhaps because it was the poorer sections of society who suffered most it was a phenomenon that was scarcely recorded. The lives of most people in the 19th century were 'nasty, brutish and short.' It is not surprising that they turned to the cheapest drug available. The irony, of course, being that this only made their situation even worse. From the late 18th century whisky overtook beer as the most popular alcoholic drink. Public houses, which were often just a room in a private house could sell spirits as well as beer. In England a separate licence was required to sell spirits. This made whisky cheaper and more readily available, and as it was eight times stronger than beer drunkenness was common. In addition to legal premises there were a vast amount of illegal shebeens and dram shops which provided drink cheaply and easily.

It was not just the cheapness and availability of alcohol which made it such a major factor in Scottish life. Drink was part of the social and cultural fabric. People drank at weddings, funerals, christenings, at New Year, at hiring fairs and most business deals were concluded with a couple of drams. This combined with poor living conditions, long hours of work helped create a climate in which drink was seen as the only opportunity to escape the harshness of everyday existence.

Drink was not the only factor in helping to create the conditions in which murderous violence occurred. Hatred and prejudice against Catholics and the Irish could end in tragedy as it did in Kelso in 1856. Then there were the individual human dramas like that so tragically played out in Ednam in 1923 and in Peebles in 1916.

Norrie McLeish
October 2000
Jedburgh

The Death of the White Knight

Broomhouse, near Duns 1517

A few months after the death of James IV on Flodden's bloody ground a small ship, accompanied by seven heavily armed French vessels, landed on the west coast of Scotland. The fleet had brought John, Duke of Albany, cousin of the dead king, back to Scotland. His return represented a triumph for those Scots nobles who wanted to have the support of France against the territorial ambitions of England.

After the disaster at Flodden, Scotland remained in a difficult and dangerous situation. James IV's widow, Margaret Tudor, sister of Henry VIII, became Regent and guardian of the infant heir to the throne. The following year she married the ambitious Earl of Angus, head of the 'Red Douglas' family who was generally recognised as an Anglophile. The marriage divided the Scottish nobility into two factions. Those who supported the marriage saw it as a way to make peace with England; those who were opposed to it, feared an increase in English influence in Scottish affairs and demanded that Margaret Tudor stand down from the Regency. They looked to France for help and particularly to Albany, whose father was a younger brother of James III. Despite Henry's large and frequent bribes to the Scottish nobility, Queen Margaret was forced to give up the Regency and Albany was invited to take her place.

The omens were not promising. Albany spoke only French and

had been reluctant to come to what he regarded as a cold, barbarous and alien country. In France he was highly regarded and had been appointed Lord High Admiral by Louis XII. Before he accepted the invitation of the Scottish Council there was some hard bargaining to be carried out. He demanded the restoration of the lands and titles that had been taken from his father. In addition, the nature and extent of his authority had to be clarified and agreed. The man to whom he entrusted these difficult negotiations was the extraordinary Anthony d'Arcy de la Bastie.

De la Bastie had served with distinction in the armies of Louis XII where he probably came to the attention of Albany. He was of particular value to Albany as an agent, as he had already spent some time in Scotland. He had been on friendly terms with James IV and had even been a guest at his wedding to Margaret Tudor. His first appearance in Scotland is mentioned in the Lord High Treasurer's accounts for November 26th 1506. The sum of thirty-four shillings was paid to "John Hertsheid, pailyson man to pass to Stirling to fetch the partition against the fechting of the Lord Hamilton and the French knight." Anthony de la Bastie came from a family with reputation for terrorism and violence. The Seigneurs de la Bastie-sur-Melons in Dauphiny, not far from Grenoble in the foothills of the French Alps, had a reputation for constant feuding with their neighbours. They also had an irritating habit of demanding tribute from any travellers who passed through their territories. Anthony was a younger son of this family. He was, for a while, a 'professional' on the European tournament circuit during which time he had issued a challenge to any knight in France, Spain, England and Scotland. The chivalrously inclined James IV was intrigued by this wandering knight and invited him to Scotland where he apparently jousted with the Lord Hamilton. The result was a no-doubt diplomatic draw. James IV, who prided himself on his physical prowess, also tested himself against the man who became known as 'The White Knight.' The treasurer's accounts for January 25, 1507 notes that "14 shillings was given to the smyth quhn the king and the French knight straik at the steddye." Perhaps De La Bastie allowed the king to win, for it is reported that he returned to France "laden with presents."

His experience of Scotland would have made him invaluable to Albany. During subsequent visits as Albany's agent he had continued to impress James with his combination of diplomatic skills and personal charm. After successfully helping to negotiate the conditions under which Albany would return to Scotland, De la Bastie was rewarded with a place on the Regent's governing council and was made responsible for the Lothians. There would have been much resentment among the rough and ready Scottish nobility at the elevation of the Frenchman whom they nicknamed "La Beaute." Not, I suspect, as a term of affection but one related to his reported preoccupation with his appearance; he was particularly proud of his golden flowing hair. More important to the Scottish nobility however, would have been the fact that he was an agent of Albany's. This greatly exasperated the ambitious Henry VIII of England. He wanted to remove Scotland from French influence and make sure he was able to pursue his continental ambitions without fear of an attack from Scotland. To this end he bribed may of the Scottish nobility to support him and also encouraged raids into the Scottish Borderlands. It was a successful policy, for it divided the Scottish nobility into two warring camps. One of the leading supporters of closer connections with England was the Earl of Angus and among his followers was the Home family of the eastern Borders.

The Homes were masters of the Eastern marches, the most powerful family in Berwickshire. The extent of their strength can still be seen in the ruins of their fortresses at Hume, Wedderburn, Fast Castle, Coldingham, Ayton and many others places. The family was descended from Cospatrick, Earl of Dunbar. At the beginning of the 16th century the head of the family was the Earl of Home who, for a time, held the post of Lord High Chamberlain. George Buchanan, the 16th century Scottish historian, described the Earl as a man whose, "disposition was more fierce than was expedient for the good of the times." The family, however, was regarded with some suspicion. They were close allies of the Douglases and there was a question mark over the part the Earl of Home had played at the battle of Flodden. At first Home had welcomed the return of Albany, but he quickly turned against him. He was involved in a conspiracy against Albany but it failed. Home and his brother, William, were persuaded to attend a meeting of the Parliament in Edinburgh where they were seized and imprisoned. On October 5th 1516, the Earl was beheaded and his younger brother executed the following day. Their goods and lands were confiscated and their heads put on display in Edinburgh. De la Bastie had already been given Dunbar Castle where the Earl's wife was imprisoned and he was also made Warden of the Eastern Marches, a post long held by the Homes. He was also given Home Castle together with other Home property.

All of this made Sir David Home of Wedderburn a very angry man. Home of Wedderburn was the senior line of the family. David Home had fought at Flodden where his father and one of his brothers had been killed. He was as fiery tempered as his late Earl and was determined to have his revenge on this Frenchman who had usurped his family's place in the Borders. However, he decided to bide his time and await an opportunity.

Albany left Scotland to visit France in May 1517. In his absence the governance of the realm was left in the hands of the "commissioners of regency." De la Bastie was a key member, responsible for the Lothians and the Merse. No doubt he had been well briefed to keep a close eye on his fellow-commissioners. On September 9th, while De la Bastie was on official business in Kelso, he was informed that William Cockburn was laying siege to Langton Castle, just outside Duns. There had been a dispute among the Cockburns over the guardianship of the young sons of Cockburn of Langton who had recently died. William Cockburn was married to the sister of David Home of Wedderburn. It is quite possible, however, that David Home actually 'stage-managed' this incident in order to entice De La Bastie into his territory. When De La Bastie summoned David Home to Kelso, Home refused to go unless he got clear assurances for his safety. The Frenchman gave these assurances and suggested that Home meet him when he was making his way back to Dunbar. Home agreed to this and met up with the Commissioner about two miles from Kelso. Wedderburn had eighteen horsemen with him while De La Bastie had a force of several hundred, mostly men from Teviotdale and the Merse together with a few Frenchmen.

The meeting started amicably enough. The Frenchman told Home that if Cockburn had a grievance he should take it to the courts. Home claimed that he had no control over Cockburn and that it had nothing to do with him. This was untrue and both men knew it. Exchanges became more heated. Home's anger grew when he realised that the resplendent steed that the Frenchman rode had previously belonged to the executed Earl. He accused De La Bastie of being behind the plot to kill the Earl. By now they had reached what was described as "the heath to the north of Fogo," close to what is now the village of Gavinton and hard by Langton Castle.

Home sent a message to the Cockburn brothers to come as quickly as possible. They announced their arrival by thundering down towards the cavalcade with loud yells of "Wedderburn! Wedderburn!" There was consternation among the commissioner's group. The men from Teviotdale decided that they did not want to get involved in a fight and turned around and headed back towards Hawick and Jedburgh. The men from the Merse joined the Homes and together they turned on the Frenchmen who were suddenly outnumbered and in a situation of considerable danger. De La Bastie tried to conciliate Home but to no avail. The Frenchman decided to make a bolt for Dunbar castle. From there he would no doubt raise a force to deal with this troublesome Border baron. De La Bastie spurred his horse and took off, with the Homes and their followers in close pursuit.

At first De La Bastie managed to pull ahead of his pursuers but his horse slowed down as the heavy, French-style trappings began to exhaust it. Despite this, he managed to cross the Cornie Ford between Langton and Duns fighting off desperate attempts to prevent him.

Perhaps he remembered, as he struggled to get across the ford, the warning he had been given by a local seer:

"If eer ye cross the Cornie Dyke
The corbies wil get yir bones to pyke."

He galloped through the outskirts of the old town of Duns situated slightly higher up than it is now, on the western slopes of Duns Law beside Duns Castle. The leading pursuer was one of Home's pages and the Frenchman continually fended him off while trying to reach the ford over the Whitadder at Broomhouse. His tired steed stumbled and fell in a boggy patch of ground, ever afterwards referred to as 'Bawtie's Bog'. De La Bastie fought off the young page but soon two of David Homes' brothers arrived. The killing of the Frenchman was swift and merciless. His head was severed from his shoulders and tied by the locks of his golden hair to a saddle. It was brought to Duns, where it was placed on a pike and put on display. Doubtless a reminder of the treatment meted out to the late Earl. De La Bastie's body was buried where it fell.

The murder of De la Bastie outraged the whole of Scotland. Only in Berwickshire, fiefdom of the Homes, was it regarded as justified. David Home and his brothers fled to England after the Scottish parliament passed a sentence of forfeiture against them. They were to return to their troubled homeland after a short period of exile. David Home however hadn't changed. He was involved in the infamous brawl in the streets of Edinburgh known as 'Cleanse the Causeway.' He also had a unique way of courting. His neighbour, Sir Andrew Blackadder had died at Flodden and Home paid court to his widow. He did this by laying siege to her castle and, after capturing it, he forced her to marry him thus gaining control of the Blackadder estates.

Albany returned to Scotland and provided a form of firm but even-handed government. The European situation changed and France found herself looking to England as an ally. Albany was recalled to France; a prospect no doubt he viewed with some pleasure. No further action was taken against the Homes

The spot where Antoine de la Bastie was slain was marked by a cairn in a field that was once a bog. Later, another grander monument was built close to the gates of Broomhouse estate and next to a bridge over the Whitadder. It reads: "In memory of Antoine Darcie, Signeur de la Bastie. A French knight who had been appointed warden of the marches instead of Lord Home, treacherously beheaded in Edinburgh. De La Bastie and his troops met Home of Wedderburn and his clan near Langton and Home accused him of being accessory to the slaughter of his chief. A fight ensued and de la Bastie slain and buried at this spot and a cairn was raised over the grave by order of Patrick Home of Broomhouse AD 1517."

Well it is one version I suppose. But it is Berwickshire. And it is Home territory.

Getting there

You leave Duns and take the A6105 towards Preston. About half a mile out there is a sign showing Broomhouse on your right. You take this road and follow it round to the left for about a mile and a half. The monument to Anthony de la Bastie is on the left hand side of the road. It is hard now to believe that such a peaceful countryside scene should have been the setting for such a brutal murder.

The De La Bastie Memorial
Broomhouse

The Murderous Minister

Spott East Lothian 1570

A few miles from Dunbar, the tiny village of Spott nestles on the north-eastern slopes of the Lammermuir Hills. Despite its small size and relative isolation, Spott has witnessed many dramatic events that were to help shape the nature of Scottish society. It was placed right in the middle of the route taken by many invading English armies, who so often turned the fertile plains of East Lothian into a desert. In 1650 General Leslie, in command of the Army of the Covenant retreated before the armies of Oliver Cromwell, but as he did so he burned crops and carried off cattle in order that there would be no supplies for the invading army. So successful was this policy that Cromwell had to turn back and head for the seaport of Dunbar. Leslie and his army followed and took up a strong position on Doon Hill just outside Spott. However, such was the power of the Scottish clergy who were convinced that their cause was just and that God would give them victory, that they prevailed upon Leslie to move down upon the enemy. The Army of the Covenant was decimated. Cromwell was convinced that it was the Lord who had delivered his enemies into his hands. The night after his victory was spent in "the house of Spott."

The village was also the scene for some of the last witch burnings in Scotland. the Kirk Session Records for October 1707 has the laconic entry, "Many witches burnt on Spott Loan." Before this, a number of

16th century clergymen were to meet with violent deaths at a rate unusual even for those unsettled times. In 1543 Robert Galbraith, described as the 'Parson of Spott," was murdered in Edinburgh. In 1571, his successor, John Hamilton, who having became Archbishop of St Andrews, was hung for his involvement in the assassination of the Regent Moray. Then of course, there was Spott's - and perhaps Scotland's most infamous minister: the Reverend John Kello who was to meet his fate on the Edinburgh gallows on October 4th 1570

In 1570 Scotland was in turmoil. Mary, Queen of Scots, had fled into England after her defeat at Langside, to the less than sisterly embrace of Queen Elizabeth. There she began the long imprisonment that was to end with her execution. The Regent Moray had been assassinated. Edinburgh Castle was held by the 'Mary's Lords' but was besieged by the 'King's Lords'. The 'King's lords wanted Mary deposed and her young son declared king. Directly related to this royal power struggle was the emergence of the new reformed church. The overthrow of the old Catholic faith was however, relatively bloodless in comparison to many other countries in Europe and with England in particular.

The early Protestant reformers were essentially practical men, less concerned with doctrine than with trying to bring spiritual care and enlightenment to people who had long been neglected. It was a formidable task they faced. Many churches were in a ruinous condition, sacraments and service were ridiculed and the poor, under-educated and often immoral priests were despised by the mass of the people. In some areas there were no churches or priests at all It was the first wave of new ministers of the reformed church who were given the task of creating that 'Godly state' so desired by John Knox and his followers. Among this new spiritual vanguard was the Reverend John Kello who was appointed minister to the parish of Spott.

John Kello was a man of relatively humble origin who probably came from the Linlithgow area where he was, for a time, the Public Notary. He was also Clerk to the St Andrews Diocese before being appointed minister to the parish of Spott in 1560. He was, by all accounts, a very able and talented man. He states that: "I was brocht up from my youth in exercise of learning and imployed my mind diligentlie to the meditation of vertue." He was one of those whom the first General Assembly of the reformed Church thought, "apt and able to minister." John Kello was married and the father of three children. His wife was affectionate and loving but not perhaps the ideal partner for an ambitious young man determined to advance his professional career and social status. He had inherited a little money that he had invested in some property in Linlithgow. Encouraged by this success he ploughed all the profits in a similar venture; buying property in and around Spott. It was a financial disaster and he soon found himself deep in debt. Suddenly, a career that had appeared so rich and full of promise, was looking bleak. In addition to this, he felt a deep resentment that the church appeared to be overlooking what he saw as his considerable talents.

He came to the conclusion that the only way to solve his problems was to become a single man once again. He set his sights on the daughter of a local laird who would bring him the social status he craved as well as a substantial dowry. This, he was later to describe, as "...the glistering promises wharwith Sathan, eftir his accustomed maner, eludit my senses."

The minister started to plan his wife's death. He informed friends and neighbours that she suffered from bouts of melancholy and that she was sometimes suicidal. In his confession he says that he was on the point of murdering his wife on several occasions, but at the last moment was overcome by remorse or ' sic terrouris', that he could not do it. He tried to poison her, pretending that she was ill. However, his wife seems to have been a robust woman and did not succumb to his poisons. Throughout all this John Kello continued to present a public face of a loving husband and of a moral leader of his flock.

On a Sunday morning in September 1570, John Kello finally succumbed to the blandishments of Satan and, according to his confession, murdered his wife. She was kneeling in the bedroom saying her prayers with her back to the door. Her husband approached her from behind and strangled her with a towel. He then tied a rope around her neck and suspended her body from a hook in the ceiling, making it appear that she had hanged herself. He then locked the front door of the house from the inside, left the key in the lock and slipped out the back door. He went to his church where, by all accounts, he delivered an exceptionally eloquent and impassioned sermon.

After the service he invited some of his friends back to his home. He expressed great consternation when the front door was found to be locked. On discovering his wife's body John Kello's grief seemed deep and genuine to all who saw him. He appeared to be particularly upset because as a suicide his wife was forbidden the normal church sacraments and her immortal soul would be doomed to torment for eternity. John Kello's appeared inconsolable in his grief.

If he had kept his nerve he would probably have got away with it. No suspicions were voiced about his wife's death being other than suicide. But there was an inner voice, perhaps it was conscience, perhaps something darker, that tormented John Kello. He went to visit a fellow minister, the Reverend Andrew Simpson, minister of Dunbar parish. He told his colleague that he was having difficulty coping with the implications of his wife's suicide. It must have been a dramatic meeting. During it the Rev. Simpson reminded Kello that when he had visited him when he was ill after the death of his wife, Kello had told him about a dream he had. "I doe remember when I visited you in time of sicknesse, yee did open unto me this visioun: that yee were carried by a grim man before the face of a terrible judge, and, to escape his furie, yee did precipitat yourself in a deep river. When his angels and messengers did follow you with two-edged swords, and even when they struck at you, you did decline and duck in the water, while in the end, by a way unknowne to you, yee did escape."

Did Andrew Simpson gaze deep into the dark soul of the troubled minister from Spott? Or was he a skilled psychologist, long before that term was known? Perhaps he already had his suspicions about the ambitious young minister. Certainly his next words to John Kello were dramatic and intense. "This vision I doe so interpret; that yee are the author yourself of this cruel murder, then conceived in your heart, and are carried before the terrible judgement of God in your own conscience which now standeth in God's presence to accuse you. The messenger of

God is the justice of the countrie, before which yee shall be presented. The water wherein yee stood is the vain hypocrisy of your own and feigned blaspheming of God's name, whereby yee purpose to colour your impiety."

John Kello's immediate reaction to this stunning denunciation must have been one of total consternation. Did he proclaim his innocence or break down in tears and confess all? On this the sources are silent. But Andrew Simpson was a stern and unbending man and demanded that the hapless minister hand himself over to the authorities. Kello contemplated fleeing the country but his conscience would have always been with him, "the terrors of the night" as he described it. More than this though; he was utterly convinced that God had spoken to him through the voice of the Reverend Andrew Simpson. It was a deeply troubled man who made his way to Edinburgh the next day to confess the murder of his wife to the church and civil authorities.

The news sent shock waves throughout the newly established Protestant church. The reformers had claimed that the old pre-Reformation clergy had been corrupt and evil. Now less than ten years after its creation one of the church's ministers was confessing to the dreadful murder of his wife and of trying to cover it up with the vilest hypocrisy. For the infant church it was a public relations disaster.

John Kello was found guilty and was sentenced to be hung. Shortly before his execution a pamphlet called "The Confessione of John Kello" was printed and distributed. In it he claimed to be extremely penitent and said that Satan had "intoxicated his mind." The church, of course, was anxious to make the most of this public penitence which showed that Satan could tempt even the "most Godly of persons." Kello declared that his wife had never given him any cause for offence and that if he got his time back again he would want to spend it with her. A commentator of the time wrote: " And thus he departtit this lyfe with an extreme penitent and contreit part, bayth for this, and all uther offences in generall to the great gude example and comfort of all the beholders, upon the 4 day of October 1570."

John Kello delivered his last sermon on the steps of the scaffold to "ane grit multitude" and "desired the people not to measure the truthe of God's word by the lives or the falls of the preachers........" After his execution his body was burnt to ashes and his goods were declared forfeit to the crown. His children, however, were to successfully appeal against this and were able to claim his goods. The awful fates of his mother and father did not seem to deter their son, Bartholomew, who was to have successful career in the church - although this was in England, not Scotland.

And so departed from this life John Kello, the murderous minister of Spott. Or was he? There is an alternative explanation though it can now never be proved. John Kello's wife may actually have committed suicide. He may have become insane through grief, remorse and guilt at having driven his wife to take her own life. His fellow minister's interpretation of his dream may have brought all these guilt feelings welling out of him and he convinced himself that he was guilty of the murder of his wife. There have been many such cases where someone in a state of mental anxiety has confessed to crimes they did not commit. Today we are much more aware of the dark workings of the human mind. In 16th century Scotland, however, it was easier to pin the blame on the devil and all his works.

Murder in the Black Bull

Jedburgh 1726

1726 was to be the final year of the reign of George I. He was the first of a line of monarchs from Germany who came to rule over a kingdom whose parliaments had united as recently as 1707. It had been hoped that the union would bring greater material prosperity to Scotland. Whatever the longer term consequences for the rest of the kingdom, the union with England was a disaster for the town of Jedburgh. Its history, economic well-being and distinctive character had been shaped by being so close to the English border. The Union of the Crowns had effectively put an end to cross-border raiding, a feature of Border life for centuries. The ruthless suppression of the 'riding' clans had brought a measure of peace to the area. No longer would the wild Turnbulls attack Jedburgh as they had in 1601, creating mayhem and bloodshed in the Market Square and murdering the town's Provost. But England and Scotland, despite the fact that they had a single monarch, were still separate countries after 1603, with different trade regulations and systems of tariffs. Many goods exported from England to Scotland and vice versa attracted tax duties. The avoidance of these duties encouraged the growth of smuggling which became a major source of profit all along the border. Jedburgh was well placed to benefit from this illegal trade in contraband goods, there being no major settlement between it and Newcastle. Despite the numerous laws governing trade,

Jedburgh became very prosperous from the export of salt, skins, cattle and malt into England without the formality of having to pay excise duties. Its prosperity was further enhanced by the illegal smuggling of goods from England and from the continent. There were many wealthy pedlars living in Jedburgh who plied their illegal trade on a daily basis. The Union of the Parliaments put an end to this illegal traffic by dissolving the Border and thus removing the need for import and export duties. The appointment of an increased number of excise officers helped decrease the smuggling of goods from the continent. As a result trade in Jedburgh languished and the town slipped into poverty. Emigration from the town increased and the population of the burgh dropped dramatically. An interesting indicator of the rate of decline is that while before 1707 there were over forty malt barns and kilns in use within the burgh boundaries, by the end of the 18th century there were only three.

1726 was an election year in Jedburgh, when a member was returned for the county of Roxburgh to sit in the parliament at Westminster. Only a few people had the right to vote and as voting was a public affair there was a great deal of bribery and corruption which flourished in the poverty which afflicted Scotland in general and the Borders in particular. Sometimes this would take the form of a straightforward offer of a cash gift or, in the case of the gentry, it could be the offer of support for a regimental commission for a second son. Once elected the new member tended to take little interest in his constituency and would immediately set about recovering the money he had laid out in getting himself elected.

In the August of that year it was widely believed that Sir Gilbert Eliott of Stobs would secure the nomination for the county seat. Sir Gilbert was the 3rd Baronet of Stobs and chief of the Elliot clan. He had served as the member of parliament for the county of Roxburgh between 1708 and 1715 and was the Chief Magistrate of the county. Despite this he lived for most of the year in a fashionable town house in Edinburgh. Much to the annoyance of Sir Gilbert, it was Scott, the Younger, of Ancrum who secured the nomination. Although the clan or tribal spirit had been greatly eroded when the Border disappeared, feelings of kinship were still strong in the Borders where little love was lost between the Elliots and the Scotts. The hostility between the families made the bitter flavour of defeat even more difficult for Sir Gilbert Eliott to swallow. So it was that a few days after the election, when Sir Gilbert came to Jedburgh in his capacity as Chief Magistrate, he was still brooding over his failure to be elected.

Among the business to be attended to that day was the drawing up of a list of electors for any subsequent elections. During this process, Sir Gilbert was subjected to numerous jibes about his defeat in the recent election. This would not have improved his ill-humour. Despite this, on the conclusion of business, Sir Gilbert was persuaded to join a company who had gathered for dinner in the large dining room on the first floor of the Black Bull Inn. Among them was Colonel John Stewart of Stewartfield. Although Colonel Stewart's father had only owned Stewartfield since 1704, his family had ancient connections with Jedburgh. He was a descendant of John Stewart of Buncle who had been killed at the battle of Falkirk in 1298 fighting alongside William Wallace. There are a number of charters from the 13th century referring to a "John Stewart de Jedburghe."

Once dinner was finished, the large company settled down, some playing at cards and some sitting talking. It was a noisy gathering with a great deal of drink being consumed. Sir Gilbert and Colonel Stewart found themselves sitting opposite each other. At first the atmosphere was described as "jollity itself" but it soon started to darken when Eliott and Stewart started to discuss recent election. The Eliotts of Stobs had a reputation for being quick-tempered and the current clan chief shared this trait. Witnesses agreed that it was Elliott who started taking out his spleen on Colonel Stewart. Colonel Stewart was heard to say that if he had done anything to affront him, he apologised for it. One of the company, a Captain Ross of the Royal Regiment of Dragoons, told them to stop talking about the elections as they were boring the rest of the company. Possibly the gallant captain, despite having consumed a prodigious amount of drink, managed to detect the growing bad blood between the two men. He tried to calm matters down but was singularly unsuccessful in his attempt to do so. The captain soon became aware that Eliott and Stewart were at each other's throats again. He heard Eliott demand to know why Stewart had not voted for him. The Colonel replied that: "He lay under a great many obligations to Sir Patrick Scott and his family and thought he could do no less than vote for Mr Scott." Sir Gilbert was far beyond accepting what appeared to be a very reasonable explanation and continued to harangue the Colonel. Captain Ross heard Stewart say, "Pray, Sir Gilbert, you have said a great deal to provoke me, do not provoke me further." The atmosphere around the two men became very tense.

What happened next is not entirely clear. Most of the witnesses were fairly drunk and the nearest witness, Captain Ross, had his attention diverted by someone across the room. He became aware that Colonel Stewart had flung a glass of wine in Sir Gilbert's face, but did not know why he had done so. Sir Gilbert leaped out of his chair with his sword unsheathed. Colonel Stewart remained seated in his chair, a stricken look on his face, his hands clasping his stomach. He gasped out that Sir Gilbert had wounded him and that he was a dog for doing so. A number of the company seized Sir Gilbert but attention was diverted to the need to help Colonel Stewart and after having had his sword taken away, Sir Gilbert was temporarily forgotten.

The commotion was heard in the downstairs rooms and one of the first to rush upstairs was George Rigg, Sir Gilbert's personal servant. He rapidly sized up the situation and grabbed hold of Sir Gilbert, urging him to leave immediately. Sir Gilbert refused, but his servant told him that the Colonel's wound was liable to be fatal. It was a shocked Sir Gilbert who allowed himself to be ushered downstairs. They were passed on their way down by the landlady, Mrs Christine Ainslie, who noted that Sir Gilbert had lost his wig and that he stumbled as he came down the stairs. Rigg took his master outside and hid him behind a tombstone in the churchyard of Jedburgh Abbey, taking care to cover him with a plaid, while he went off to fetch horses from a nearby stable. When he returned both men mounted and galloped off into the night. After spending the night in a nearby forest Sir Gilbert managed to find a ship which took him and his servant off to Holland.

Colonel Stewart was carried into the landlord's private chambers and a surgeon was summoned. When Andrew Rutherford, the surgeon, arrived, Colonel Stewart was lying "with his head bare, his coatt oppen and his shirt bloody." He told the surgeon that Elliott had murdered him as he was sitting in his chair. The fatally wounded man was moved to Stewartfield where he died a few days later. A meeting of the county magistrates was convened which was attended by the dead man's son and by John Scott of Ancrum for whom Stewart had voted in the recent election. A warrant was issued for the arrest of Sir Gilbert Elliott.

But Sir Gilbert had friends and kinsmen in high places. Lord Minto, who was also Lord of Session was an Elliott. William Elliott of Wells was a wealthy merchant in the city of London; as well as being a kinsman, he was also Sir Gilbert's father-in-law. The connections of Lord Minto and the wealth of William Elliott combined to obtain Sir Gilbert a full pardon and he returned from exile after a short time. However,the murder of Colonel John Stewart was to cast a dark shadow over the rest of his life. His wife died shortly after his return. He sold his Edinburgh property and retired from public life. Becoming something of a recluse, he devoted the rest of his long life to family affairs and the management of his estate. He died in 1764.

Colonel Stewart's son succeeded to Stewartfield but he did not stay in Jedburgh for long. Perhaps the injustice of his father's death rankled, but for whatever reason the long connection between the Stewarts and Jedburgh was over. In 1845 the name of the estate was changed to Hartrigge and the last remaining link of the Stewart family with the town of Jedburgh had disappeared forever.

Getting There

If you come down the A68 from Edinburgh you turn right into Jedburgh Town centre. There is a large car park on the left hand side. On leaving the car park you can walk up the Canongate which in 1726 was the main street in Jedburgh and which looks very different today from what it did then. Down on the river is the Auld Brig which was once the main entry into the town and across which Charles Edward

Stuart led his Jacobite army in 1745. From there he would have ridden up the Canongate watched no doubt by curious , but not very welcoming, Jedburgh citizens.

A little way up on the right hand side of the Canongate are Shaws newsagents and the Brown Sugar restaurant. These now occupy the site of the Black Bull Inn with stables at the rear. Colonel Stewart was killed in one of the upstairs rooms

Site of Black Bull Inn

The Murder of Lady Billie

Eyemouth, August 1751

The ancient mansion of Linthill stands on the road to Ayton a few miles outside the Berwickshire fishing village of Eyemouth. According to local legend it is a place long associated with ghosts and hauntings. Numerous residents claimed that they they had heard a phantom carriage draw up outside, this was followed by the noise of doors opening and closing and footsteps clattering up the stairs as if carrying a heavy weight. Then came what sounded like something being laid on the floor. Locals said that 'the heavy weight' was the body of a young man who had been 'out' in the Jacobite rising of 1715. He was mortally wounded in the skirmish and this was him being brought home to die. Ghosts,we are told, are supposed to be linked with places where great emotional traumas have been suffered. If this is true then Linthill deserves to be the haunt of ghosts quite different from those of young Jacobite lairds.

In 1751 Linthill was home to Lady Home, the widow of the Reverend Ninian Home who had abandoned his work as a Church of Scotland minister to carve out a highly lucrative career in buying and selling property. At one time he had boasted that he would buy up the whole of the Merse and was referred to by the locals as 'Ringham the Conqueror'. He was deposed in 1716 as minister of Sprouston parish for what was described as his "untender and unministerial conduct" which probably included his support of the Jacobite rising in 1715. Included in the property that he purchased was the estate of Billie in the neighbouring parish of Bunkle as well as the mansion of Linthill. Ninian Home died in 1744. His son was to use the proceeds of his father's worldly endeavours to build the stately Paxton House which has recently been opened to the public.

Lady Billie lived on in the Linthill mansion after her husband's death. Her husband had made himself rather unpopular during his lifetime and, as a result, his widow found herself relatively friendless but surrounded by a considerable number of servants at Linthill. Her most trusted confidant was her butler Norman Ross who originally came from Inverness and who had been with the family for many years.

It was the custom of Lady Billie to personally collect the rent from her numerous tenants. She went round the district with Norman Ross who helped her count it and store it away in a strong box in her bedroom. It should be remembered that banks were few and far between in these days and people had to take precautions to look after their money which they normally kept in the house. Lady Billie had quite an ingenious device constructed to protect her cash by securing the door to her bedroom. A heavy brass cylinder was allowed to fall into an opening in the door. The opening had been designed so that the cylinder fitted exactly into it. A cord was attached to the eye in the cylinder and from there it ran on to a pulley linked to running blocks close to Lady Billie's bedside. The old lady was thus able to bolt or unbolt the door without having to get out of bed and no one was able to enter the room while the bolt was down. Norman Ross of course was entirely familiar with this arrangement.

On Monday evening on the 12th of August 1751 Norman Ross concealed himself in Lady Billie's bedroom while she was out walking with her grandchildren. When she returned she had supper in her bedroom with her grandchildren and then retired for the night. Throughout the supper with the children, Norman Ross stood silently in his hiding place. He heard Lady Billie undress, get into bed and then pull down the cylinder cord which locked her door for the night. Unbeknown to her however, Norman Ross had placed some cherry stones in the opening which would have allowed him to leave the room when he wanted to without disturbing Lady Billie. When he thought Lady Billie was asleep, the butler emerged from his hiding place and approached her bed to get hold of the keys which she kept under her pillow. As he approached the bed the old lady suddenly sat up and demanded to know who was there. Ross panicked. There was a struggle in which the old lady fought furiously. Ross stumbled around the room and took hold of a knife that had been used for the supper and which was lying on the bedroom table. What kind of subconscious rage, resentment and bitterness overtook Ross at that moment we shall never know. He attacked Lady Billie with the knife and inflicted terrible injuries on her. The old lady fought gamely and tenaciously for her life. At one point she managed to seize hold of the knife cutting her hands badly in the process. Finally, he cut her throat and left her lying on the bed. He seized hold of the keys to the strong box and was trying to unlock this when he heard a noise behind him. He turned and saw a blood-covered Lady Billie reaching out and groping for the bell cord. Ross launched himself at her but was too late to prevent her from pulling the cord and raising the alarm. The bell rang out as Norman Ross stood over the bed on which his mistress had collapsed unconscious. He heard the sound of servants starting to climb the stairs. There seemed no way out. There was a great clamour outside the bedroom door and, in desperation, he launched himself out of the window and crashed on to the drive below. Norman Ross was not a particularly athletic individual and was rather on the stout side. He landed badly and broke his leg. Almost overcome by pain and panic he managed to drag himself through the garden and into a field of barley beside the house. He was to lie there for four days.

Lady Billie lingered for a few days, long enough to give a detailed statement of what had happened and confirm the identity of her attacker. She died on the 16th of August. Meanwhile a manhunt for Norman Ross had been set in motion throughout the countryside. The brutal murder of Lady Billie had sent a shiver of fear through the stately homes of many of the landed gentry and made them glance somewhat askance at their trusted servants. It was not any strong personal sense of loss that made them determined to catch her murderer. They were determined to show that no member of the servant class could get away with such a heinous crime.

For four long hot days Norman Ross lay in growing fear and terrible pain in the field alongside the house. At last overcome by thirst, he made his way down to a burn at the foot of the field. Two small children were playing happily a little further up the burn when they saw this matted, wild-eyed creature crawling out of the field. They fled in terror and told their parents. Norman Ross was swiftly captured and unceremoniously carried off to prison in Edinburgh.

He appeared before Edinburgh High Court on the 11th of November 1751 and was tried for the murder of Lady Billie. Throughout the trial he denied that he had murdered his mistress. The jury decided otherwise and found him guilty and sentenced him to death. Later, as he lay in prison awaiting his, fate he confessed to the murder though he insisted that his motive had been robbery and that he had never intended to kill Lady Billie. He said that a local girl had borne his child the previous summer and that she was pressing him for money. He had borrowed money from friends to help support the child and that it was only because he was in desperate straits that he was tempted to steal. He claimed that the girl was the cause of all his woes and warned that it was necessary, "....to guard against the least sins, because one sin follows another as materially as the shadow does the body."

The execution was carried out on the 10th of January 1752 at Gallowlee between Edinburgh and Leith. As was the practice in those days, his right hand was chopped off before he was hung. His body was then hung with chains wrapped around it and his hand stuck on top of the gallows. Presumably the audience watched this with a mixture of edification and terror!

The aftermaths of the deaths of both victim and murderer had elements of both the farcical and the macabre. At the funeral of Lady Billie the party arrived at Bunkle graveyard only to discover that they had left the corpse behind. As Scottish funerals of the time were noted for the amount of drink that was consumed this was probably a contributory factor to the company's forgetfulness. When she was eventually interred Lady Billie lay under a flat stone with no inscription to indicate that she was there.

Even more macabre is the story surrounding Ross's body. It is said that a drunken butcher, by the name of Nichol Brown, laid a wager with his companions that he could cut a slice of the corpse's thigh, fry it and eat it. This he proceeded to do and afterwards got so drunk that he attacked and murdered his wife when he got home. He apparently ended up being hung on the same gallows as Norman Ross.

The crime was remembered in Berwickshire for a long time after the details had been forgotten, preserved in a children's nursery rhyme:

"The Lady's gane and Norman's ta'en,
Norman wi' the bloody hand,
Now he will have to pay the kain
For being at the Deil's command

Norman Ross wi pykit pow
Three corbies at his e'en;
Girnin in the gallows tow,
Sic a sight was never seen".

Getting There

Linthill stands a little way along the B6335 on the road to Eyemouth after turning off the A1. It stands in an elevated position on the left hand side a little way off the road. The tale of Norman Ross and the murder of Lady Billie is one well-known in the district

Linthill

Bad Day at Greystonelees

Ayton, 24th September 1772

1772 was not a good year for the tenants of the farm of Greystonelees. Archibald Rule, the tenant, and his son Alexander had struggled to make a success of their holding situated right on the edge of the land overlooking the grey North Sea. But the land had been harsh and unforgiving, providing little reward for long years of hard labour. On Sunday the 24th September, it appeared that their struggles had ended in failure. Over the years their debts had mounted and now they were anticipating a visit from the sheriff officers who would begin the process of sequestration against the Rule family. The day had started bleakly but it was to become even worse. It was late evening and the darkening was gathering when three men rode into Greystonelees farm.

The three, grim-looking horsemen were George Smith, a merchant in Greenlaw, Alexander Christie, writer in Greenlaw and Robert Hamilton, sheriff officer from Duns. All three were men of respectable station in Berwickshire. What exactly took place after they arrived will probably never be entirely known. The records show two conflicting accounts. But the events that followed on that Sunday in Greystonelees were to result in a death followed by an extraordinary lengthy legal episode which was to last for five years.

According to the three men, young Alexander Rule had launched a totally unprovoked and violent attack on them. They claimed they had merely held him off and delivered some minor blows in self-defence. He had, they said, walked away from them back to his house. They were to point out that he had been ill for some time with jaundice. Apparently he had contracted a fever the next day and had died four days later. His death, they were eager to point out, had nothing to do with them.

This version of events seems to have been accepted. During the subsequent enquiry into the circumstances surrounding Alexander Rule's death, a statement was read from his father. In it he declared that; "there had been no malicious intention on the part of the pannells, but merely a scuffle in which the young man was the aggressor and that there was no foundation for a trial for murder." That would appear to have brought the whole unhappy episode to an end. The fact that Archibald Rule could neither read nor write was not regarded as having any significance. It would appear that the three men could breathe easily; but it was not to be. The events of that September evening were to come back to haunt them.

Four years after the death of his son, Archibald Rule put his mark to a petition to the Lords of Justiciary asking to have the three men imprisoned on suspicion of murder. The petition claimed that the three men had evaded justice through "illegal devices." One of these "illegal devices" was forcing the father to sign statements including one, "binding himself never to bring a prosecution against the pannells, in the full knowledge that Archibald Rule could not read."

The account of the events of that fateful evening four years before, that was given in the petition, was very different from that which had originally been accepted. The three men had arrived at Graystonelees at sunset. After a short argument with Alexander Rule, they violently attacked him with whips and sticks. They knocked him to the ground and 'lay upon him, bruised him and crushed him in a barbarous and inhumane manner." A number of people in the vicinity saw the attack and called on them to stop. Young Janet White, who was walking along the sea-braes, was horrified at what she saw and tried to get them to stop. They ignored her and continued to beat the young man. She heard them calling on God to "damn Alexander's soul" and far from showing any signs of compassion, they urged each other on with cries of, "Knock him on the head!" and "kill him!" Eventually they tired, mounted their horses and rode off into the gathering gloom. Alexander Rule was left lying in a pool of his own blood. His father helped him to his feet and held his son as they made their way, slowly and painstakingly, back to their house. The boy was vomiting blood and was put to bed. He developed a raging fever and died a few days later. Up until that fateful day Alexander Rule had kept in good health.

The solicitors of the three men named in the petition expressed outrage. They claimed that the father of the dead man had been put up to it by one James Gilkie, " a man very well known to the judges upon other occasions and who now appeared as agent in this prosecution." They said that he had taken out criminal letters without the authorisation of Archibald Rule and demanded that the petition should be dismissed out of hand. Mr Gilkie was a well-known troublemaker who was stirring things up for his own ends. The prosecution said that this was not so. "It was only after repeated applications that Mr Gilkie had undertaken to take up the prosecution." His conduct, they said, "was not only blameless, but praiseworthy."

Whether he was a troublemaker or a genuine seeker of justice; James Gilkie was soon in trouble. Shortly after he had presented the petition, he found himself in the debtor's prison. These were for debts, he said " that were not justly due." He saw the hands of Messrs Smith Hamilton and Christie in this as they were not without influence in Berwickshire society. They were, he was to claim, trying to get him to withdraw the charges "through the horrors of the dungeon." But Gilkie had friends too and soon found himself a free man. He continued to fight for a trial. "Why were the pannells not insisting on a trial to clear their names if they were as innocent of the deadly deed as they claimed," he argued.

The petition was presented to the Lords of Session who had to decide whether there was sufficient legal basis for a trial. The Lord Advocate said that in his view there was no basis to charge the men with murder and that he thought it very strange that Archibald Rule had not taken action, "when his sorrow was green." Lord Gardenstown however, said that it was a very remarkable case and that it required more investigation. He said he had a very high regard for the Lord Advocate but, "Whenever a man's life is taken away from him there should be a trial. Life is the first object of our attention, property only secondary. It is for the benefit of the innocent to be acquitted and the guilty should be brought to punishment." He declared that, " A trial should always be granted when it is insisted on by one who has a proper interest e.g the father."

The trial started before Lord Gardenstown at Jedburgh in the spring of 1777, five years after the untimely death of Alexander Rule. The defence claimed that there was no case to answer and that the father, "...was satisfied and would have continued to be so, had he not been instigated by the noted James Gilkie, a man very well known to the judges upon other occasions, and who now appeared as agent on this prosecution." They pointed out that Gilkie had "prevailed with Archibald Rule to sign a petition praying to have the pannells incarcerated for murder, committed some time ago." They pointed out that, when Lord Hailes had read the petition, he had expressed his displeasure in the strongest possible terms at the length of time that had passed. They also read out the father's disclaimers of the criminal letters in which he stated that he would never bring a criminal prosecution against the pannells. Under these circumstances the defence argued that the case should be dismissed.

The prosecution claimed that the pannells had used what they described as 'artful endeavours' and had withheld evidence to stop this case coming to trial. They said it was quite wrong to suggest that Archibald Rule was satisfied, and that he fully supported and authorised the prosecution of the three men. If, they argued, "they were as innocent as they claimed to be, why did they not put themselves forward for a fair trial - instead they had tried to elude justice by illegal devices."

"It was," said Lord Gardenstown, "a remarkable case." He then stated that the trial could not proceed at present as the defence had trusted to their deposition and had not called up witnesses. He did remark, however, that he did not find it incredible that the father had signed a document without being aware of the contents. It was always open to him to retract it in court. He concluded with a thinly veiled warning' "If Mr Gilkie has stirred up this prosecution, solely from a love of public justice, he must have a very pure mind. I hope he has."

The new trial started on the 23rd June 1777. The defence immediately went on the attack. They pointed out that the Lord Advocate had said there was no case to answer, that a discharge had been signed by Archibald Rule and that the length of time between the alleged assault and the trial was too long. They also made much of what they claimed to be the improper conduct of James Gilkie. They said he had been publishing pamphlets which gave an unfavourable impression of the accused to the general public. However, they were conscious of their innocence and would waive any legal objections to allowing the trial to proceed on one condition. That was that Archibald Rule would hand in security for their expenses if they were found, as they fully expected to be, 'not guilty.' No doubt they were fully aware that neither Archibald Rule nor Gilkie could afford to hand in such security. Mr Gilkie protested and said that if this was accepted then it would prove an 'insurmountable barrier'. The court, thought otherwise. They were highly critical of Mr Gilkie's conduct after the criminal letters had been raised. However, they said that if Archibald Rule wanted to execute a new indictment against the pannells he could do so. But of course he could not afford to even consider such possible costs.

The affair ended in a whimper. Gilkie acknowledged his fault and threw himself at the mercy of the court. He said he had been over-zealous for his employer, Mr Rule, and had wanted to hit back at those defaming him. He was sentenced to one month's imprisonment.

It is difficult now to decide if James Gilkie was a staunch seeker after justice or merely a trouble maker intent on using poor Archibald Rule as a way of getting at his enemies. Or was it the case of the county gentry covering up a dreadful crime against a poor man who was powerless to obtain justice? The real truth of what happened on that long ago day on the little farm by the grey North Sea will probably never be known. But even now a father's grief at the death of his son can still echo down the centuries.

Getting There

Greystonelees farm stands alongside the A1 overlooking the North Sea, once known as the German Ocean. Leaving Berwick-upon-Tweed you head up the A1 towards Edinburgh. Greystonelees farm is on the left hand side about three miles up the road before the turn-off to Ayton.

Greystonelees Farm Today

Murder in the Mill Port

Hawick 1814

Hawick's last execution took place at the Common Haugh on Thursday 12th May 1814. John Gibson, a nail maker, was hanged for the murder of his wife in the Mill Port the previous November. The execution was a mixture of public entertainment and a display of the solemn and terrible majesty of the law. It also provided an opportunity for the church to impress upon the population the awful consequences of the evils of drink.

Originally from Ayr, John Gibson married Janet Renwick, the daughter of Gideon Renwick, a Hawick butcher, in April 1795. He had met Janet when he was billeted with the Renwick family while serving in the army. After their marriage, Janet accompanied her husband to various postings throughout Scotland and Ireland. During this time it was said that she experienced a life of 'great hardship' and gave birth to three children, all of whom died. The couple were to have another eight children, "eleven pledges of our mutual regard," as John Gibson was later to describe them. Only two girls and a boy were to survive however. Gibson left the army and set up in business as a nail maker in Hawick. However, after a particularly heavy drinking session in Edinburgh he found that he had signed himself back in the army. He deserted, and spent the next four years trying to evade the military authorities, living at various times in Longtown, Ireland and Newcastle.

In Newcastle he was press-ganged into the navy but managed to jump ship in London and from there walked back to Hawick. For a while he settled in Langholm and later Kelso along with Janet and their surviving children. However, his luck had run out, for the military authorities caught up with him and he was arrested and taken to Aberdeen. Janet travelled to Aberdeen and made an eloquent and emotional plea for mercy. As a result of this he escaped punishment but had to remain in the army until 1809 after which he returned to Hawick. As soon as he got back he was promptly rearrested and charged with desertion from the navy and taken to Jedburgh jail. In his written testament he said that, "Ministers, Magistrates, and the whole town of Hawick felt very much interested for me." He claimed that they petitioned the authorities saying he was, "sober, industrious, well-behaved and deserving news of my discharge." It must have worked for he was quickly released.

A number of witnesses attested to the fact that the couple had been happily married for fourteen years. The same witnesses also claimed that Janet was a respectable woman, but this picture of domestic respectability was somewhat spoilt by John Gibson's claim that their last child was not his. He said that the father was a French officer, who was a family friend and a frequent visitor to their house.

Britain had been at war with France for a number of years and prisoners of war were billeted in Hawick as well as in other Border towns. In November 1812 there were 120 officers from Napoleon's army in Hawick. They must have seemed an exotic breed to the citizens of the Borders, these young officers in their bright, but often threadbare uniforms. They opened cafes, organised concerts and some augmented their incomes by setting up as teachers of dancing. No doubt they proved to be as much of an attraction to Hawick's young ladies as the free-spending American GIs were to be to the girls in many British towns during WW2. It was commented that, "The presence of so many well-dressed persons for so long a period produced a marked reform in the costume of the inhabitants of Hawick." They were relatively free to come and go as they pleased and as friendships developed with the townsfolk, no doubt a number of more intimate relationships also blossomed. Whether this was the case with Janet Renwick is in some doubt - after giving birth to so many children one wonders where she got the energy!

Infidelity was not the only complaint that John Gibson had to make about his wife. He claimed that she was trying to poison him, administering small doses over a period of time. She was being encouraged in this, he claimed, by his wife's parents with whom he was in dispute over a share in some property.

On the evening of the 19th of November 1813, John Gibson said that he had retired to bed about ten o'clock. His wife had gone to bed earlier after an argument which had not been resolved. He described himself as, "being in body and mind very disordered." He then went on to say that he was woken up in the early hours of the morning and saw a man, whom he thought was a Frenchman, in the room with himself and his wife. He got up but could not find him. He went back to bed. A little later he felt thirsty and asked his wife to get him a drink of water. She refused. He got out of bed to get the water himself and as he did so, his wife got up and launched herself into an attack on him, seizing him by the throat. He claimed that she was trying to choke him and that he could not make her let go. In desperation he picked up his penknife and stabbed her in the throat. Her grip on his throat relaxed and with blood pouring out of her she fell to the floor .

John Brook, a stocking maker, who lived above the Gibsons, heard screaming but put this down to some soldiers who were lodging in the house at the time. The presence of these soldiers was to provide a bizarre aftermath to the story, as we shall see. Eventually John Brooks got up to see what was happening. On coming out of his door, he met a neighbour who told him that John Gibson had murdered his wife. Brooks confronted the distraught nail maker who at first said that a Frenchman had done it, but then admitted that he had murdered his wife and that he had intended to kill himself as well. In his evidence at Gibson's trial, John Brook stated that he thought that Gibson was jealous of his wife's relationship with the French officer. The Sheriff Officer was summoned and John Gibson again confessed his guilt, saying, "I murdered her and meant to have done the same to myself but I will now let that alone, yet I will have to die for it."

During his trial, presided over by Lord Gillies, a Jedburgh surgeon stated that, "The prisoner suffered from a considerable degree of melancholy but not to such an extent as to prevent him from knowing that murder was a crime". It did not take the jury long to bring in a unanimous verdict of 'Guilty'! Lord Gillies passed the sentence: "the prisoner should be fed upon bread and water until the 12th of May next .... and between the hours of two and four in the afternoon of that day, be hanged by the common executioner on a gibbet until he was dead, in the town of Hawick." It was said that Gibson appeared totally resigned to his fate as his sentence was read out. However, a number of observers were pleased to report, that after the trial, thanks to the remonstrations of the local minister, John Gibson had become suitably penitent.

On the morning of the execution John Gibson emerged from the prison in Jedburgh, clutching a bible and escorted by the local minister. He was accompanied by Jedburgh's Provost and Magistrates along with the entire town guard of about seventy men to a spot called Bergess Sla, about a mile from the town. There he was formally handed over to the Sheriff of Roxburgh and a troop of the Roxburgh Yeomanry cavalry. Gibson was placed in an open cart and the procession started off on its long journey to Hawick.

The entire route was packed with people from all the surrounding villages and farms, curious to see the man who was about to meet his maker on that day. When they came into Hawick the party, now joined by the Hawick magistrates and officiating clergy, made its way to the town house. It was from there, a short time later, that John Gibson made his final journey through the streets of the ancient town. With the Sheriff and Magistrates, he made his solemn way down to the Common Haugh. In front of him was the band of the local Roxburgh Militia playing, appropriately enough, 'The Dead March'. Two companies of the local militia were lined up along the road from the Teviot Bridge to the Common Haugh. The authorities were conscious that so many people were packed into the streets and, particularly in the Common Haugh, that there was a very real danger of public disorder. But it was to be a solemn and silent audience that met the procession when it arrived at the Haugh.

As he ascended the scaffold Gibson joined with the officiating clergyman in singing the hymn, "The Hour of my Departure is Come". He then addressed the crowd saying, "since my condemnation, a great many lies have been circulated about me, the authors of which I entirely forgive. I am now on the brink of eternity, and with the awful prospect before me I can certainly say that I never materially injured man or woman, but my own family, for which I am now to suffer. I now warn all who hear to beware of any excessive drink or passion - to these causes I owe my unhappy fate." He then stood for a moment in the middle of the scaffold, silent and with his head bent. After a few moments the Sheriff gently reminded him that it was almost time. He climbed the ladder to the drop with a firmness and composure which impressed all who saw him. He signalled to the executioner and took the plunge into eternity.

In a biographical pamphlet issued at the time of the hanging, John Gibson says little about what happened on the fatal night. He wrote that, he wants "to draw a veil over the events of that dreadful night. I had hardly committed the horrid deed, when the remembrance of her long continued kindness to me rushed upon my mind...."

Given the weight of evidence, together with his own confession it appears that the case against John Gibson was quite clear cut, although it could be argued that he was mentally unbalanced at the time. The Frenchman whom he had suspected of being his wife's lover had, along with his fellow prisoners-of-war, returned to France before the trial. However, three years after the execution of John Gibson, an ex-soldier, James Barnes, who was being transported to Australia for another crime, confessed to the murder of a woman in Hawick in December 1814. The sheriff in Hawick passed the relevant papers on to the Secretary of State who appears to have taken no action.

There was a party of soldiers passing through Hawick on the night of the murder and some of them spent the night in the building where Gibson and his family lived. Could one of them have entered the Gibson's apartment and committed the murder? Could a mentally distraught and guilt-ridden Gibson have convinced himself that he had killed his wife? There is probably more to this story than will ever come to light. Perhaps part of the truth may could have been revealed by eleven year old Gideon Gibson, who wanted to make a statement about "the murder of his mother." Significantly it was the prosecution who successfully argued that his evidence was inadmissible on the grounds of his age. In a final plea to the people of Hawick, John Gibson wrote, "Let me die in the hope that none possessed of human feelings will scowl upon my poor children, nor add to their sorrow by casting in their teeth the untimely end of their unfortunate father."

Getting There

The execution of John Gibson took place at Hawick's town Haugh. The gallows are supposed to have stood on the spot now occupied by a car showroom at the foot of Commercial Road,

At the southern end of the High Street just before it sweeps round to the Sandbed you can find the Mill Port. When you walk down the narrow wynd it takes you out along the banks of the Teviot. In the early part of the 19th century it had a reputation as a place of cheap lodging houses. It was probably in one of these that the Gibson family lived.

A Death at the Fair

Kelso August 1856

As far as the locals were concerned, the great Fair of St James had 'Aye been!' Held, it seemed, from time immemorial on the same green tongue of land formed by the Tweed and the Teviot where these two legendary Border rivers meet at Kelso. Originally it had been the market fair for the great, lost burgh of Roxburgh, which at one time was as important as Edinburgh, Aberdeen and Dundee. It had been a thriving, prosperous hive of activity when Glasgow was but a village. The Fair was held on the Festival of St James the Apostle who was the patron saint of the burgh of Roxburgh. The great burgh fell victim to the ravages of the Wars of Independence with hardly any of it remaining to be seen today. But the Fair continued and was one of the most important in the south of Scotland. It was where the people of the Borders went to buy linen, cheese, wool, ready-made clothes and shoes, as well as for the purchase of sheep, cattle and horses. By the beginning of the 19th century the nature of the Fair was beginning to change. Although some business was still transacted, labourers hired for the harvest and gypsies sold crockery, it became more and more a place for pleasure. People went to the Fair to drink whisky and ale, eat gingerbread, meet old friends, be entertained and sometimes be parted from their hard-earned cash by hucksters and pickpockets who were attracted by the large numbers of people gathered there. By 1856 St James Fair had become an annual event where people went mainly to enjoy themselves.

In 1856 the Fair also attracted large numbers of railway workers. Railways were springing up all over the country and their construction was made possible by thousands of Irish labourers or 'navvies.' These workers were young, single, Irishmen who were attracted to the physically demanding and often dangerous work as they could earn much more than they could in their own impoverished homeland. There had, however, been a long history of hostility between Border people and the Irish incomers. For over half a century workers from Ireland had been coming to the Borders to work at he harvest. Harvest time was when many Borderers looked to earn a little extra to supplement their meagre incomes. The arrival of the Irish who were prepared to work for much less, effectively removed a source of income for many labourers and caused them to resent the incomers. Ethnic and linguistic differences between the Lowland Scot and the Irish were added to by the fact that the Irish were practically all Roman Catholics. In 1849 Ireland suffered a dreadful famine as a result of the failure of the potato crop. There was a dramatic increase in the number of Irish emigrants in the following years. When rail tracks began to be laid in the Borders, large numbers of Irish labourers descended on its quiet towns and villages. Many of these young Irishmen were only there to earn enough money to take them to America which they regarded as the real land of opportunity. The Borders regarded the Irish with suspicion and hostility. The Irish, in their view, were only interested in brawling and fighting and consuming vast amounts of whisky. The Irish, in turn, felt that they were being exploited by the unfriendly Borderers and tended to stay together in camps and large groups for protection in what they considered to be a hostile environment. Occasionally these tensions would explode in an orgy of violence as it had done at the St Boswell Fair a few years previously. The memory of that day of riot and murder, however, was not uppermost in the minds of Borders folk as they prepared for another St James Fair on the 5th August 1856. They were quite unaware that by the end of that long, hot summer's day a young man would lose his life and that the normally peaceful town of Kelso would be subjected to a night of arson and terror.

The summer's heat had attracted large crowds of people to the Fair. The stalls and merry-go -rounds were busy. Although numerous pickpockets and card sharps were also busy, on the whole, most people were enjoying themselves. However, there had been complaints about a crowd of rowdy Irishmen who had been boisterous and noisy and generally making a nuisance of themselves. By evening, when the air had turned muggy, many of them were drunk as were some of the younger elements of the townsfolk. What had originally been mere verbal abuse developed into a series of running fights. Soon a number of Kelso men had taken over the lower end of the fair and, armed with sticks, attacked any Irishman who ventured near. The Irish armed themselves in a similar fashion and soon a full-scale brawl broke out with both sides laying into each other without restraint.

The fighting raged for about an hour with over a hundred men involved. At one point, when the battle was at its most most intense, an Irishman wrenched up a tent-pole and struck out wildly at a group of local youths, knocking one of them to the ground. As he lay on the ground an Irishman, dressed in a black coat and brown trousers, sat across the chest of the fallen man. He had the unconscious youth by the hair and was banging his head off the ground. After a while he was pulled off the man by some of his compatriots, leaving the man still lying unconscious with blood flowing from his head. When the fighting died down a few minutes later, a doctor was summoned. A quick inspection revealed that the young man was past all help and was clearly dead.

Earlier that evening Robert Mills, a 25 year old tanner who lived in Roxburgh Street, was making his way home from the Fair, with his wife and children. He had been working in the morning and had spent the afternoon at the Fair with his family. As the day wore on the children had become fretful in the heat and Mrs Mills became concerned at the number of drunken fights that had broken out. They decided to make their way home. About halfway home Robert suddenly said that he wanted to go back to the Fair. He gave no reason but said that he would be no longer than fifteen minutes. Despite her protestations he set off back, turning only once to wave to his family. Later that day Mrs Mills was to declare that she "never saw him again in life." It was Robert Mills whose prone body was to be found lying beaten and battered on the ground at St James' Fair.

It was always going to be difficult for the authorities to determine whether Robert Mills had died as a result of the blow from the tent-pole or because of the repeated banging of his head on the ground. There had been much noise and confusion during the fight and many potential witnesses were somewhat the worse for drink. In addition to this, many of the Irish were reluctant to give information to a police force which they regarded as prejudiced against them. The identity of the man who struck Robert Mills with the tent-pole was never properly established but, after extensive interviews, the police identified a suspect as the man who had so brutally beaten Robert Mills. He was Thomas Burke, an Irish hawker, who had lived for a while in the village of Kirk Yetholm. But Thomas Burke was nowhere to be found; in the confusion following the attack he had quietly and quickly left the Fair.

News of the killing of Robert Mills, and the circumstances surrounding it, spread like wildfire throughout Kelso and the wider Borders. No doubt the truth became somewhat distorted in the telling and retelling. Be that as it may, there was no doubting the reaction to the death of the young Kelso man. All the pent-up rage against the Irish burst out in an orgy of destruction and violence which affected many otherwise law-abiding citizens. Any Irish on the streets or in the vicinity of Kelso were liable to be attacked. Many who were still at the Fair fled in terror leaving their goods and belongings behind. Hugh Ferguson who was camping just outside Kirk Yetholm found himself confronted by an angry mob of local people and was forced to wield an iron bar to defend himself and his family. The next day the unhealthy excitement became even worse. The hostility against the Irish developed into a hostility against Catholics and spread far beyond Kelso. It was reported that in Jedburgh, local Catholics gathered together anything they had of value and placed themselves under the protection of the Sheriff. This was later denied by an indignant Jedburgh citizen who claimed that Jeddart folk were much more tolerant of their Catholic brethren than their neighbours in Kelso! He was to write, "...if the proceedings at Kelso had been attempted, the community would not have awaited until midnight, but at the first symptom of such an outrage would have risen as one man and inflicted summary and condign punishment on the miserable and misguided creatures." In the village of Kirk Yetholm 'the king of the gypsies' decreed that all Irish had twenty-four hours to leave. The few foolhardy souls who remained after the allotted time were chased for miles over the hills by an angry mob of gypsies.

On that day there was a sale of cattle in the Market Place. But talk was as much about the death of Robert Mills as it was about the price of cattle. A palpable air of tension hung over the town all day. Jane Byrne was the schoolmistress at the small school attached to the Catholic chapel which was situated at the end of Roxburgh and Bowmont streets opposite the Dukes Gate. Jane had been warned that there were rumours that the chapel was to be burned down. Jane Byrne slept in a small room at the side of the chapel, but she wisely accepted the invitation to move in with some friends for that night.

As the day progressed and no firm arrests had been made, the mood of the town turned uglier. By early evening, a large crowd had gathered in the square and despite the efforts of the police, few showed any inclination to leave. Many in the crowd were angry and excited, some were there as expectant observers, all were waiting for something to happen. Suddenly there was a series of whistles and, as if this had been a prearranged signal, the crowd moved purposefully off. They split into two columns and marched in parallel lines down Bowmont Street and Roxburgh Street, heading towards the Catholic Chapel. As the two columns of angry townsfolk arrived at the Chapel, another mob arrived from the other end of town. It was, for all the world, like a well-executed military operation.

Two lone policeman stood on guard outside the chapel. It must have been a nerve-wracking time for them to be confronted by such a large and ferocious mob. Suddenly a hail of stones poured down on them and they had to retreat for fear of their lives, followed by much jeering and catcalls. The crowd surged forward and some of them broke in to the chapel, ransacking it and drinking the sacramental wine. The

Chapel was then set alight and as the fire raged through the building there were cries of delight from the crowd. Police reinforcements arrived but the crowd prevented them from getting near the building. Among the interested spectators were some of the most respectable citizens of Kelso. The local magistrates, however, were greatly alarmed at the turn events were taking. The town bell was rung and the Riot Act read. The crowd was ordered to disperse but many remained to watch the Chapel burn to the ground.

The news of the riot caused feelings of outrage throughout Scotland. The Edinburgh Courant commented, "....we sincerely hope that the riot at Kelso will be the last occurrence of this kind which will disgrace the annals of this country." The lack of police action in preventing the burning of the chapel, especially when it had been widely discussed the day before, came in for particular criticism. They had apparently made no effort to recover any of the property stolen from the chapel. Stung by this the local magistrates pressed for action. A number of young men were arrested but only three came to trial. They were Alexander Orr, Patrick Jeffrey and Thomas Little who were regarded as being the ring leaders of the mob. A local newspaper however, commented that, "the hands of justice had grabbed some idle simpletons."

The three were charged with mobbing and rioting and wilful fire raising. These were serious charges which could carry a sentence of transportation. They pled 'not guilty' to all charges. The evidence of the police made it clear that they had all been part of the riot and that they were there until the chapel had been burned to the ground. What was not clear was whether or not they were ringleaders in the rioting and burning. In his directions to the jury, the judge made it clear that,".....everyone who encourages, aids, participates, or takes any part in the common object of a mob, whatever that part may be, is equally guilty of the results of the acts committed by that mob..."

Despite this, the jury returned a verdict of 'not proven' on the charge of arson but 'guilty of mobbing and rioting.' The jury also made a unanimous plea for leniency as, " the mobbing and rioting might have been prevented if there had been a sufficient police force in Kelso." The judge was obviously not impressed by the verdict. He thought that there was little difference in being part of the mob which set fire to the chapel and actually carrying out the act of arson. However, he went on, no doubt ironically, "the jury had seen fit to make that decision." He also made it very clear that if they had been found guilty of arson they would have been transported. He sentenced the three to 18 months hard labour. The verdict was received with an air of indifference by the men in the dock. I would suspect that air of indifference covered up a strong sense of relief.

And what of the man or men responsible for the murder of Robert Mills? The police arrested a few men but had to release them. It took some time for the identity of the main suspect, Thomas Burke, to be established and a warrant for his arrest to be issued. The man who had disappeared into the crowd that fateful, hot August afternoon had walked out of the Fair. He was last heard of sailing for America. There he vanished into that sprawling, developing country. Perhaps his descendants have prospered and have no knowledge of their ancestor's role in the grim tragedy played out at St James Fair on that hot summer evening so long ago.

Getting There

Although St James Fair ceased many years ago, it has a successor in the Borders Union Agricultural Show which is held every August in the same place as the Fair was held. It is a place where business is conducted and where old friends can socialise. It is however, much more sedate and trouble-free than the old St James's Fairs ever were.

High Street, Coldstream
As Alexander Thomson would have known known it

A Mild Mannered Man

Coldstream December 1864

Set in a sheltered position on the north bank of the Tweed, mid-19th century Coldstream was a prosperous little town. For travellers from England, coming up by the eastern route and heading inland, it was the first stop on the Scottish side of the Border. The Border crossing was made over an imposing and attractive bridge designed by Smeaton the engineer, and opened in 1766. Its construction encouraged a number of hopeful young lovers to cross over to take advantage of the lower legal age for marriage in Scotland. The Coldstream Bridge Toll House became celebrated as the site of many runaway weddings, including those of no less than four future English Lord Chancellors. In time, a lucrative trade in the celebration of marriages was to develop which rivalled that of its western counterpart - Gretna Green. It was not only English young lovers who came to Coldstream to marry. Many of the young country people from Berwickshire and Northumberland plighted their troth in the Toll House. For them it was a romantic undertaking though it certainly was not regarded as such by the Church of Scotland, whose ministers consistently denounced this fashion for these "irregular marriages." By the mid-19th century however, Coldstream had become a prosperous small town, with an air of gentle Victorian respectability.

In December 1864 one of Coldstream's 'weel-kent' citizens was Alexander Thomson who had a china shop on the High Street. As well as running the shop, Thomson made and sold fishing tackle and looked after the account books of a local medical firm. Born in nearby Duns, he had left to seek his fortune in London where he was, for a while, employed in a shipping firm. Shortly after his marriage in 1852 to Margaret Dickson, he came back to Berwickshire and opened the china shop in Coldstream. Alexander Thomson was a well-educated man with many friends among the respectable people of Coldstream. Although by no means wealthy, he was highly regarded and was generally looked upon as a pleasant man of a kindly disposition. The Thomsons set up home in a tenement building in Church Close, which was situated between the High Street and Market Street. They were the only people who lived in the Close, the other tenements being used as stores by the merchants of the town. This humble accommodation hardly reflected the education and social standing of Alexander Thomson. It was all he could afford however, for Thomson had a major problem with alcohol which dominated his life and was ultimately to lead to tragedy and horror.

For many years alcoholism was regarded as the result of some kind of moral lapse on the part of the individual. Later it was regarded by some as a self-destructive response to an individual's psychological or social problems. Some view the condition as a disease. Not all heavy drinkers become alcoholics and there is now considerable evidence that it may be a genetically determined condition. It is a chronic, progressive illness. It is thus very difficult for the individual to bring about a cure by themselves. If there is still some disagreement over the causes of alcoholism, then there is widespread agreement over its effects. It takes over all aspects of the sufferer's life; emotional and social as well as physical and mental.

Excessive drinking can lead to vitamin deficiency, together with damage to the liver and central nervous system. Withdrawal symptoms can be severe; the worst being delirium tremens which can involve fevers, hallucinations and often total disorientation. The ability to concentrate and act effectively is impaired. Bad temper, jealousy and paranoid delusions are not uncommon. Emotionally, the problem drinker becomes very unpredictable; violent outbursts may be followed by periods of guilt and introspection. These feelings of guilt however, are not strong enough to make the drinker change. At its worst the desire for alcohol takes over completely. Everything else becomes subservient to the need to meet this craving, including family, friends and even religion. Alexander Thomson showed all the symptoms of a problem drinker at his worst.

It would appear that Thomson was a binge drinker. He could go for several months without touching a drop. He had married in 1852 and it was reported that he had managed to stay away from alcohol for a period of three years. In the intervals between drinking bouts he was an intelligent, pleasant man, a regular attender at the United Presbyterian Church. Under the influence of alcohol however, he was described as acting like a "mad person." In 1855, 1862 and 1864 he suffered severe attacks of 'delirium tremens.' During these periods he "exhibited an inordinate desire for drink." So strong was this desire that his friends acquired a strait-jacket to restrain him and sometimes borrowed leg-irons from the local police station in order to prevent him going out to buy drink. Alexander Thomson was fortunate to have so many friends in the community,as well as having a supportive wife, prepared to help him despite the noisy and abusive behaviour he displayed when he was drunk.

In October 1863 there occurred an incident that should have been of concern to his friends. His wife had become afraid of him when he was very drunk and claimed that he had threatened her. In self-defence she had struck him with a poker. His reaction was to go berserk and destroy all the furniture in the house after his wife had fled. He was, said a local doctor, "stark mad."

In the middle of November 1863 Alexander Thomson started on a drinking binge which was to end in horror three weeks later. During this period he had been physically restrained by the application of the straitjacket. Several people commented, that Thomson seemed depressed and unhappy and that he had talked of committing suicide. Not surprisingly his business was suffering and this was weighing heavily upon him. By the first weekend in December it appeared to many that he was more stable. However, on Sunday the 4th he drank steadily all day and his mood so alarmed his wife that she hid all the knives and razors in the house. At seven o'clock that evening Thomson went to bed. He promised his wife that he was better and she agreed that he should not be straitjacketed. She did however, take away and hide his clothes as an insurance that he would not get up and go out to find drink. Some friends had come to help his wife. They left shortly after seven o'clock with Thomson, to all intents and purposes, sleeping as soundly as baby.

Andrew Donaldson, the sheriff officer in Coldstream, lived close to Thomson's house. About six o'clock on the Sunday morning he was awakened by the sound of a frantic banging on his front door. He got up and opened the door to be confronted by Alexander Thomson wearing only socks and a shirt which was tied round his middle like a lady's petticoat. Donaldson noticed that the shirt was smeared with blood. Thomson was shivering with cold and his eyes were fixed and staring. In a feeble voice and half-crying he said to the astonished sheriff officer, "I've killed Margaret. I've come to give myself in Andrew." Andrew Donaldson got dressed and with some foreboding accompanied the distraught Thomson back to his two-apartment house. He was totally unprepared for the scene of carnage that met him when he entered the kitchen. Margaret Dickson's body was lying on the floor, her feet towards the bed. She had suffered dreadful injuries. It was later established that she had six broken ribs on either side of her body, some of them had been driven into her lungs, from the ferocity of the attack made upon her. Her head was lacerated with deep wounds. A post-mortem examination was to reveal that Margaret Dickson could have died from either the head or chest wounds. The state of the room showed that a fearful struggle had taken place; the floor and bedclothes were saturated with blood and furniture was broken and scattered about. Donaldson called a neighbour to summon the police. He noticed a poker and a pair of tongs smeared with blood and hair, lying on the floor. A crude attempt had been made to clean the blood off the floor. All this time a dazed Alexander Thomson stood and gazed around him, a blank expression on his face, seeming to be hardly aware of the carnage around him.

He was taken to Greenlaw Jail and, on the way there, announced several times that he wanted to kill himself. So concerned was the magistrate about this threat that he ordered that two constables should keep close watch over him. During that night he claimed that there were people in the cell who were trying to harm him. The prison surgeon was summoned and stated that Thomson was suffering a severe attack of 'delirium tremens.' No doubt his conscience was also beginning to increase his distress.

Alexander Thomson made a lengthy statement in which he declared that he was 42 years of age and had been married for 12 years. He said that he was subject to bouts of hard drinking and that when he was sober he could not remember anything that happened when he was drunk. He said that he had been drinking heavily on Sunday 4th December but could not remember where he had obtained the drink. He said that he had had no quarrel with his wife that night and had come to about 11 o'clock dressed only on his shirt. His wife was in bed in the other room. He could recall telling his wife that he was very dry and that he drank two bottles of ale but did not know whether she had given him them or not. He went to the water pipe with a jug in his hand to get a drink of water when, he said, his wife jumped out of bed and told him that she was leaving him. He recalled saying to her that it would never do for her to leave him and that if she tried to do so he would hit her with the jug, but added that he had no intention of doing so. At this point his wife had rushed at him and he accidentally hit her on the head with the jug. She seized hold of the poker and struck him several times with it. He took the poker from her, laid it down, and went to bed. He came to again about five in the morning. He went into the kitchen and found his wife lying underneath the bed. She said she was unwell and could not get out. He managed to pull her out and lay her on the bed but she rolled off onto the floor. It was then that he went out to fetch Doctor Turnbull but he was away and he went to Andrew Donaldson's house. He said that to the best of his recollection he had not struck his wife either with poker or tongs, but only with a jug.

The trial of Alexander Thomson took place at the High Court in Jedburgh in May 1865. He was described as a quiet, inoffensive looking , grey-haired man who looked much older than his 42 years. When he first entered the dock, he was clearly in an agitated state but, as the trial progressed, he became calmer and listened to the evidence with great interest. It was only when the blood-stained bedclothes were produced that he appeared visibly shaken. The prosecution said that there were three questions for the jury to consider. Did Margaret Dickson die of the wounds inflicted on her? Did Alexander Thomson kill her? Was he insane at the time? The first two of these questions were easily answered. The third was more contentious. The prosecution stated that it was for the defence to show that Thomson was insane at the time and that, in their view, this meant that there was a "total destruction of reason." It was also pointed out that drunkenness was not an excuse and the fact that he could remember details showed that he was responsible for his actions. The defence had Dr Tuke, Medical Officer at Morningside Asylum, who said that, "absence of motive, the strangely violent character of his conduct and his giving himself up to justice would lead me to suppose he was suffering from an attack of acute mania." In his summing up the Judge, Lord Ardmillan, told the jury that there was no doubt that Thomson had committed the deed. What they had to do was make a distinction between a state of insane mind and a state of furious rage. An insane mind he defined as one in which there was an "absolute alienation of reason." He pointed out that the medical evidence, together with what they had heard about the prisoner's history suggested insanity. However, the prisoner's statement and recollections did not favour the insanity theory. His case would probably have been stronger if he had not stated that his wife had struck him with the poker. He reminded the jury that although it was likely that an attack of 'delirium tremens' had brought on the violent attack; they had to be convinced that the defence had proved this.

The jury was out for half an hour. He was found 'not guilty' by a unanimous verdict, "in respect that when he committed the crime he was temporarily insane." Thomson, who had been gazing at the floor, looked up when the verdict was announced. A tear rolled down his cheek. As the jury left the court he bowed to them. Lord Ardmillan then announced that the prisoner should be confined to Greenlaw Jail until, "Her Majesty's pleasure in respect to him was known."

Getting There

If you come into Coldstream from Edinburgh down the A697 you pass along the High Street. On the right hand side you will see Market Street which leads down to Market Square and the Coldstream Guards museum. The next opening , which you are likely to miss unless you are on foot, leads us into Church Close. On the right is the Church of Scotland and a little further in is an empty grain warehouse. It is a pleasant enough place on a sunny summer's day but on a cold, dank December evening the gathering shadows help to create an atmosphere in which it is not difficult to imagine that this is a place where somethng horrible has occurred.

The Church was built in 1906 and the house where the murder of Margaret Thompson took place was probably situated on the site of the Church.

Old St Boswells

The Body in the Well

St Boswells 12th August 1869.

Alexander Imery, innkeeper of the Buccleuch Arms in St Boswells, stretched out his arms and enjoyed the early morning sun. It promised to be as hot as it had been on the previous few days in that August of 1869. It was only four o'clock in the morning but Alexander could see Jessie Davidson, who lived opposite, on the other side of the Edinburgh Road and across St Boswells Green, already busily scrubbing away at her board, a pile of laundry beside her. He gave her a wave which she returned with a cheery grin. He had known Jessie from when she was a little girl and knew her to be a hard working woman. "It is a pity," he thought to himself, "that she has such a problem with liquor." He watched for a moment as Jessie continued with her scrubbing. He looked up at the sky, savoured the fresh warmth of the morning for one last time before going indoors. "It was certainly going to be hot — too hot," he reckoned. "There will be a thunderstorm before the day is through,"he said to himself as he went indoors. Across the Green, Jessie Davidson paused, wiped some of the sweat from her eyes and then returned to her scrubbing.

Jessie Davidson had been born and raised in the village of St Boswells, or Lesudden as it was known locally. She was Jessie Rankine then, until she married 26 year old John Davidson in 1859. For the first few months of their marriage they had lived in Kelso and then for a while in the Toll House in the village of Maxton until eventually they returned to St Boswells and had lived there for about five years, her husband worked as a fisherman. It was not the steadiest of jobs and to supplement their income Jessie took in laundry. After ten years of marriage the couple had no children. This may well have been a contributory factor to the problems that were to beset their marriage. It was not the whole answer, however, for they had been married less than a year and a half when Jessie first left her husband and went back to live with her parents having accused him of beating and abusing her. After six months she was eventually persuaded to return but the beatings continued. In Victorian Scotland the marriage vow of 'for better or worse' was strictly enforced on working class women who had little choice but to endure the 'worse'. She told a number of her relatives and friends that she was sure that her husband was going to kill her. On one occasion she complained to her sister-in-law that John Davidson had dragged her downstairs by the hair. On another evening she had arrived at her brother's house distraught, with her face covered in blood, claiming that her husband was chasing her with a hatchet and threatening to murder her. Some of her neighbours had seen the bruises on her body which she said had been the result of beatings by her husband. Her family and a few of her neighbours were aware that Jessie had a drink problem. Whether the problem existed before her marriage or whether it came about as a result of the state of her marriage combined with her childlessness, we shall never know. They did not look for such explanations to account for human behaviour in those days. But Jessie did drink and it did undoubtedly exacerbate many of the tensions that already existed between her and her husband. They tried to hide the drinking and the violence, for at least a veneer of respectability was important if one wanted to live socially with neighbours in the village community.

It was not only Jessie Rankine's day that had started early that morning. In the warm days of summer, village life and work started when the sun came up. She was seen by a number of villagers before eight o'clock most of whom claimed that she appeared perfectly sober. It was to be in the interests of the defence at the subsequent trial to establish that Jessie was in fact very drunk for most of that morning.

That she had been drinking was undeniable but, certainly to all outward appearances, it did not seem to have affected her. Around half past five,when she had finished some of her laundry work, she went to Mrs Wales' public house where she tried to get some whisky but was refused, not because it was so early in the morning but because of Jessie's reputation. About an hour later she went into the Buccleuch Arms and asked Alexander Imery for some whisky. He also refused her, but when she complained of feeling unwell he gave her a small whisky and told her she should have it with some warm water. A little later she called again at the back door of the inn, where she saw her friend Isabella Motion, who was a cook in the hotel. There she had what the cook described, as "her usual nip." She then returned to her work with the laundry until just after nine o' clock. Shortly afterwards Helen Adams, the police constable's wife, was passing the Davidson's door and was invited into the house by Jessie. When she went in she found that John Davidson was also there. He appeared to be very agitated and said that Jessie had been getting drink from somewhere and that he had to take a bottle away from her. Helen Adams did not get the impression that Jessie was any the worse for drink. Jessie told her husband to hold his tongue and not shame her in front of a neighbour. Mrs Adams, somewhat embarrassed by this little confrontation, decided to leave. Two hours later Jessie turned up at her house and asked if she could borrow sixpence from her. As Mrs Adams' husband had left strict instructions that under no circumstances had she to lend Jessie any money, she had to refuse. She also noticed that this time Jessie seemed very much the worse for drink. Not in the least put out by her refusal, Jessie sat down and said to the policeman's wife, "Well I will repay you all I owe you if I live; but I dare say I will not live long in the world, for I am fair tired of it." It was a remark the defence was to make much of. As they were sitting talking both women saw John Davidson passing the window. "There's John looking for me but just let him seek." She added that it was her husband who had sent her to borrow the sixpence and that he would be furious when she returned without it. Jessie Rankine left shortly afterwards. Helen Adams was never to see her alive again.

Twenty-two year old Janet McGregor was a servant to Mr and Mrs Charles Ogilvie who had rented the house next to the Davidsons. Charles Ogilvie was an Edinburgh accountant who regularly spent his summer holiday in St. Boswells. Janet had seen Jessie several times that morning and it had struck her that Jessie seemed to be "going out and in" of the house much more than usual. She automatically assumed that Jessie had been drinking as she was one of those aware of Jessie's liking for hard liquor. She saw John Davidson for the last time that morning, sometime between eleven and noon as he came out from the garden with some potatoes in his hands. A little later she saw Jessie in the garden and noticed she had something in her hand, but could not see what it was and was not, according to her testimony, taking a great deal of notice. Mrs Ogilvie was in the garden just after midday and saw Jessie with a bundle of washing in her arms. Mrs Ogilvie remarked how hot it was. Jessie agreed and squinted at the sky saying that she thought there might be thunder and carried on her way, apparently to hang up the washing on the line which was next to an old disused well at the bottom of her neighbour's garden.

About one o'clock, Jessie Godfrey saw John Davidson leaning over the old well in the Adams's garden. The well had not been in use for some years and an old door had been placed over it with some heavy stones on top to stop children from removing it. Later she was prepared to swear that the door was still on top of the well, though the stones had been moved, when she first saw John Davidson there. He was leaning over the well with a rope with a cleek attached to it and appeared to be trying to get something from the well. Mrs Godfrey asked if he had lost anything to which he replied, without looking round, "a pitcher". But almost immediately he cried out to the startled Mrs Godfrey, "My wife! My wife!" He shouted at Mrs Godfrey to fetch some help.

Charles Ogilvie was upstairs when he heard his wife calling on him. "Oh Charles! Come quick! Davidson's wife's in the well!" He hurried out and ran down to the end of the footpath where he saw Davidson leaning over the well with a rope in his hand. The door was no longer over the well. John Davidson looked up and cried, "Oh sir! It's my wife in the well!" Charles Ogilvie peered over Davidson's shoulder. The water was about five feet from the top of the well and he could see the back of Jessie's head. Davidson's hook had caught in her dress but he was unable to pull her from the water by himself. Within minutes a number of villagers had arrived and with their help Charles Ogilvie was able to get Jessie out of the well. He laid her down on her side in a sloping position with the head raised to let the water run out of her mouth. He felt for a pulse or a heartbeat. There was none. Her eyes were open but they were fixed and staring. Charles Ogilvie had no doubt that Jessie Davidson was dead. He noticed that Jessie had a deep wound on the left side of her temple. John Davidson started to cry and called out, "Jessie, Jessie! You've made a bad end o' yourself. You see what cursed drink has done." He covered his face in his hands and started to sob. The body of Jessie Davidson was placed on the door that had covered the well and was carried in to her house.

An immediate investigation was launched into the circumstances surrounding Jessie Davidson's death. It was to be almost two weeks, however, before the Procurator Fiscal ordered that John Davidson be taken into custody and charged with the murder of his wife. It was only as he gradually gathered evidence from the villagers of John Davidson's history of violence towards his wife that he decided that there was a case to answer.

The trial of John Davidson took place at the High Court in Jedburgh on September twenty-fifth 1869. It was presided over by the Lord Justice General and Lord Jerviswood. At ten o'clock that morning the presiding judges led a solemn procession from the Spread Eagle Hotel to the court watched by a large crowd despite the heavy rain. Among the members of the procession were the Sheriffs of the Border counties and the Provost and Magistrates of Jedburgh. The full and awesome ritual of the law was being brought to bear on John Davidson. It did not seem to disconcert him, however, for, when the charge of murder was read out to him, he said 'not guilty' in a strong, clear voice. He was to maintain this calm demeanour throughout the trial which took place in a crowded courtroom. John Davidson was a stoutly made man, about five feet six inches tall. As he stood in the dock and gazed around the courtroom, he found that he himself was the object of intense interest from the well-dressed ladies who crowded the gallery.

The indictment was read out. It stated that "on the 12th of August last in a garden near St Boswells, in the shire of Roxburgh, occupied by Alexander Adams, police constable, residing in St Boswells, and which garden is distant about 46 yards to the south or south east of a dwelling house or premises, lately occupied by Elizabeth Imery, then, or now, or lately residing there, said John Davidson did wickedly and feloniously attack Jessie Rankine or Davidson, his wife, then residing with him in St Boswells, and did seize hold of her, and push or throw her into a well situate in or near the garden above libelled; and the said John Davidson did previously evince malice and ill-will against the said Jessie Rankine or Davidson."

The prosecution, led by the Advocate Depute, quickly established the pattern of violence which John Davidson had exhibited towards his wife. The defence, led by Messrs. Watson and Young, was equally quick to fix in the jurors' minds the fact that Jessie Davidson was much given to drink. The events of that fateful morning were outlined with the prosecution making much of Jessie's intoxication and depressed state of mind. The defence, on the other hand, cited the police witness who claimed that Mrs Davidson could not possibly have gone into the well through the small gap left between the door and the walls of the well. The medical evidence was divided between whether the wound on Jessie's temple had been caused by a blow or a fall. However, both the doctors called agreed that it had been caused by an impact of considerable violence.

The declaration of John Davidson, giving his account of what had happened was read out to the court. He said that he and his wife had lived very happily together and were very fond of each other. On the morning in question, his wife had got up about four o'clock to do a washing. He had got up about three hours later and immediately became aware that his wife had been drinking. She had, he said, been drinking steadily for the last fortnight. He watched his wife go across to the inn opposite the house to get some milk. She was there for about ten minutes. He saw her leave by a back door and take a footpath down into the village when he lost sight of her. When she returned about nine o'clock she told him that she had been kept waiting for the milk. She went to a press or cupboard and took something from it. When he asked her what it was, she replied that it was something to make him watch her. He discovered it was a corkscrew and took it from her. Jessie stormed out of the house and John Davidson watched her as she climbed over a fence and into a field. She returned about half an hour later very much the worse for drink. She tried to continue with her work but could not settle to it and kept on going in and out of the house. About twelve o'clock she lifted up a basket of clothes which she had washed and left the house to hang the clothes out to dry - or so John Davidson assumed. He told her he would pick some potatoes for the dinner and went out and started to do so. Jessie came back about five minutes later with a towel in her hands. She gave him, what he described as a vacant stare and left the house without saying a word to him. After a while he went out to see what she was doing. He saw two pairs of sheets hanging on the ropes with the rest of the washing still in the basket on a wall beside the drying ropes. His wife was nowhere to be seen. He went back to the house and cooked and ate a few of the potatoes but felt uneasy. He went out to look for her again. As he passed the well he noticed that two of the stones had been removed from one side of the door. This had caused the door to be raised a little at one end so that he could see inside the well. He saw some green scum and pieces of bark floating on top of the water. It did not seem to have been disturbed so he returned to the house. The fact that two of the stones had been moved, however, continued to worry him and he decided to search the well again. He took his rope and cleek with him. When Mrs Godfrey had called to him he had not caught hold of anything and that is why he told her that he was looking for a pitcher; but almost immediately he had snagged his wife's petticoat.

In his summing-up the Advocate Depute stated that "If the case is one of suicide it is certainly a most remarkable one if the deceased had crept in at the aperture referred to by several witnesses". He pointed out that she would have had great difficulty getting into the well and reminded the jury of police evidence which firmly stated that it would have been impossible for Jessie Davidson to have squeezed through the gap between the door and the well. He also stressed the fact that the wound on the temple was a very severe one and that it could only have been caused if "she had been flung violently into the well". The surface of the water was only five feet below the top of the well and, he pointed out, Jessie Davidson was a sparsely-built woman.

In their summing-up the defence pointed out that the well was situated close to houses where there were often a number of people about and suggested it was a most unlikely place to commit a murder. They also highlighted the fact that no one had seen Davidson and his wife together in the garden. Nor had anyone seen any signs of a struggle around the well nor had anyone heard a cry. Medical evidence, they continued, had established that the cut on Jessie's temple had been caused by the fall into the well and not by a blow with a blunt instrument, which, the jury were reminded, had never been found despite an intensive search.

In his address to the jury, the Lord Justice General stated that there was not the slightest evidence to prove malice or felonious intent on the part of the prisoner. There was also no doubt that the deceased had met her death by drowning. Her death, he observed, could only have happened in one of three ways. She could have been forced into it and if that was the case it was clearly an act of murder. She could have committed suicide and he reminded the jury that a number of people had remarked on the fact that the deceased had been in a 'morbid state of mind' for some time. It could also have been an accident when she may have slipped and fallen into the well. He went on to remind the jury that it was not for them to speculate on how she got into the well but for the prosecution to prove that she was forced into it. He also observed "that a murderer who did an act of pushing a body into a well generally selected one which was in an unfrequented situation; but the prisoner seemed not only to have rendered himself to the gaze of others, but even to court observation. Unless", he stated, "the jury were convinced that there was substantial and satisfactory proof that the prisoner committed the deed with his own hands, they must give in a verdict of acquittal."

That was enough for the jury who were only out for about seven minutes before they came back into the overcrowded and sweltering courtroom to deliver a verdict of "not guilty". The packed spectators immediately burst into loud cheers, led by the well-dressed ladies in the gallery but this outburst was quickly quelled by the court officials. As he came down from the dock John Davidson shook the hands of his father and of the defence officials and walked from the court a free man.

The verdict of course meant that in the eyes of the law he was innocent of the crime of murder. What bothers me, however, is the unfinished washing. Jessie Davidson was described by several witnesses as a hard and conscientious worker. It seems odd that she only hung up half her washing before throwing herself into the well. It seems to me that she would either not have started it or have completed it unless, of course, she was interrupted in the middle of it!

John Davidson continued to live in the village of St Boswells where he found employment as a letter carrier. The local people must have accepted the verdict although no doubt some had their reservations. It would appear that there was greater sympathy towards a man who had a wife with a drink problem than there was towards a wife who was regularly beaten by her husband. He was not to survive his wife long however; six years after Jessie's death John Davidson died at the age of forty three from a disease of the lungs. He never remarried.

The Davidson affair was once the scandal of the neighbourhood; it provided material for gossip and speculation for many years. But the years passed. The well was removed. John Davidson and those who remembered him died or moved away. In a short time few remembered much about the sad death of Jessie Davidson.

Getting There

The Buccleuch Arms still stands opposite the village green in St Boswells village right on the A68. The exact location of the Davidson house has been a bit more difficult to place. Old maps show a well beside the houses immediately opposite the Buccleuch Arms. It is likely that the well was situated in the area currently bounded by a hedge in front of one of the houses. There would have been a terraced row of houses situated here. Hardly a trace remains of the spot where poor Jessie Davidson met her sad and mysterious end.

Site of the Commercial Hotel, Earlston

A Morning's Shooting

Earlston 12th December 1877

It was a crisp winter's morning in the small Berwickshire town of Earlston situated thirty one miles from Edinburgh and seven miles from Lauder. It was a bustling, busy little place typical of many small towns that served an agricultural hinterland in the latter decades of the 19th century. It has a rather greater claim to fame in the annals of Scottish national legend; Earlston was the home of that mysterious and enigmatic figure of Scottish history known as 'Thomas the Rhymer'. 'Thomas the Rhymer' or Thomas Learmonth of Ercildoune, became famous for his prophecies and Earlston justly celebrated its fame as his birthplace and home. As life and commerce in the Borders became very difficult from the wars of independence to the union of the crowns in 1603, Earlston was all but forgotten and the legend of the Rhymer grew dim but was never entirely lost. In the centuries after the pacification of the Border, Earlston settled down to its role as a busy little market town still closely in touch with the seasonal work patterns of the countryside around it.

Wednesday the 12th December 1877 dawned like any other day for the folk of Earlston. As the morning progressed, people went about the daily routine of their lives: rising and preparing for work, getting ready for school, performing household chores and generally carrying out the many tasks that made up the uneventful pattern of their mornings.

This was not to be like other mornings, however, for the stillness was broken by the sharp cracks of gunshot fire. Those in the vicinity stopped what they were doing when they heard them. Andrew Murdison, the local slater, was in the backyard of his house when he heard what he later said was a single shot. His wife, Janet, was making the bed upstairs when she heard what she thought were two shots. Ann McWilliam, a widow who lived in the High Street, was in her bedroom when she heard a gunshot rapidly followed by another one. Catherine Falside, who lived next to the Commercial Hotel in the High Street, was scrubbing her fireside when the sound of the shots caused her to pause and look out the window. The local blacksmith, Walter Dalgleish, whose smithy backed on to the Commercial Hotel was shoeing a horse when he heard the shots ring out. All of them looked towards the source of the gunshots which appeared to be the Commercial Hotel.

The landlady of the Commercial Hotel was forty-year old Mrs. Euphemia Johnston whose first husband, Alexander Waugh, had been the tenant of the hotel until his death in 1873. Before coming to Earlston the Waughs had, for many years, run the Red Lion Hotel in the village of Heiton just outside Kelso. Euphemia Johnston was a tall woman of prepossessing appearance in a matronly way much admired by her customers and neighbours. She had continued the tenancy of the hotel after the death of her husband. In July 1875 she married one of her customers, John Johnston, a local horse dealer. He was a convivial fellow, fond of a drink and not particularly given to hard work. He was forty-six years old of medium height with a swarthy complexion. Marriage to the landlady of the Commercial Hotel must have had its attractions for him beyond that of female companionship. For someone fond of a drink and not too keen on physical effort, to become husband of a hotel landlady must have seemed like a dream come true. It is more difficult to discern what the appeal of such a marriage was for the Widow Waugh. Logic and rationality have never played a strong part when human beings choose their mates. She may have been lonely or had need of a strong and able hand to help her run the hotel or maybe she simply fell for John Johnston's rough charm. Whatever the reason for her marriage, Mrs. Johnson was a sober and industrious person with a pleasant manner and a kind heart according to her neighbours. She could also, they said, have a sharp tongue for anyone who aroused her anger but this did not happen often. In addition to herself and her husband there were seven other people living in the hotel. There were the five children of Mrs. Johnston's first marriage, the oldest of whom was eighteen year old Grace who helped her mother in the hotel. There was two year old Thomas Johnston, the only child of John and Euphemia. In addition there was a servant girl, nineteen year old Susan McGuire, who had only come down to the 'Lowlands' from her native Orkney eighteen months before.

Euphemia Johnston was several months pregnant with her husband's second child, of which the rest of the household were unaware.

The first two years of their marriage seem to have been relatively content, even though John Johnston did not do much work and continued to drink heavily. He had a short temper but his anger never lasted for very long. He kept some horses in the stables which he was always intending to hire out but he never quite got round to advertising this fact. Euphemia Johnston constantly complained that they cost money to feed but was fobbed off with the promise that he would sell them. He never seemed to get round to doing this either and on that December morning his horses were still in the stable behind the Commercial Hotel. Although this caused a certain amount of aggravation the marriage survived amiably enough. However in the autumn of 1877 the relationship between the couple deteriorated alarmingly, according to friends and neighbours. The reason for this deterioration was not hard to find. The tenancy of the hotel was coming up for renewal and John Johnston demanded that the lease be transferred to his name. His wife would not hear of such a thing and several people witnessed the couple quarrelling bitterly over the matter on a number of occasions. It may well be that the difference of opinion signified much deeper flaws in the Johnstons' relationship - lack of trust, a gradual growing apart or perhaps a dawning realisation on Euphemia Johnston's part that she had made a terrible mistake. Certainly it would appear that Johnston's indolence and his drinking habits were beginning to exasperate his wife. Instead of reacting positively and trying to save his marriage, Johnston became more surly and morose and started drinking more heavily than ever. His relationship with his step-children, which had been amiable enough up to then, also began to fray at the edges. Grace was to claim that she had heard him threaten to shoot her mother and she began to criticise him while he complained to neighbours of her impudent and abusive behaviour towards him. Whatever the reasons, tensions in the Johnston family had steadily been increasing in the weeks before that fateful December morning.

On the previous evening, Grace had been to see some friends in Melrose. When she returned she could hear raised voices in the parlour. Mr Wilson, a local grain merchant, had come to collect payment for a £20 account. Most of this was for for bran for the cows and corn for Mr Johnston's horses. Mrs Johnston refused to pay for the corn claiming that the horses were costing too much and not bringing in any revenue. Grace reckoned her stepfather was rather stupid with drink and also that he was very angry and was complaining that her mother was trying to make a fool of him.

There was little trace of the domestic tensions at the breakfast table the next morning. The young children had eaten and had been shepherded off to school. After they had gone John Johnston sat down with his wife and step-daughter to have breakfast in the kitchen. Neither Grace nor Susan McGuire, who was working in the kitchen at the time, would later recall anything untoward happening or being said during breakfast. There were no arguments and the conversation was cordial, if not affectionate, during the meal. Johnston had a bandaged thumb and Mrs Johnston had to cut his food for him. After breakfast, Grace went into the parlour where John Johnston had been sleeping in order to make up his bed. Mrs. Johnston made up the bed in her own bedroom with the help of Susan. This task complete, Susan went into the back room and started to dust it. There was a window in this room which looked out into the back court and it was while she was working there that a shot rang out quickly followed by another.

Grace heard the shots as she was making up the bed in the parlour. Immediately she ran into the backyard. She saw her mother lying stretched out with a pool of blood welling out around her head.

Running over to her Grace screamed, "Oh mother! Are you dead?" She knelt down beside her mother's prone body, looked up and saw her stepfather standing in the door of the harness room in the act of reloading his gun with a ramrod. He stared straight at Grace with what she described as a "cruel sort of look". Convinced that he was going to shoot her, Grace screamed and ran into the house and out into the High Street closely followed by the now hysterical Susan McGuire.

Andrew Murdison ran out on to the street when he heard the shots followed by the screams. He almost collided with Grace and Susan who continued to scream hysterically. Murdison pushed passed them into the hotel and through to the backyard. Johnston was still standing in front of the harness room, holding his gun and staring at the body of his wife. Scarcely believing what his eyes were telling him Andrew Murdison took in the scene. No words were spoken. Johnston stared at Murdison with eyes that the slater later described as being like "those of a cat about to spring on its prey". Certain that Johnston was going to shoot him, Murdison turned and ran back through the hotel and into the street. Grace had followed him in and, despite her panic, had the presence of mind to bolt the back door and prevent Johnston from coming into the house after them.

By this time the High Street was beginning to fill up with people who were wondering what all the commotion was about. Ann McWilliam bumped into an excited Andrew Murdison, still breathless from his terrifying confrontation with Johnston. When she asked what was going on, Andrew blurted out, "Mrs. Johnston's shot! She's clean dead!" This news spread rapidly through the crowd but the ripple of excited comment was hushed as Johnston himself emerged from the side entrance of the hotel and walked through the front door without giving a single glance towards the hushed crowd. He was not carrying his gun and this probably gave Andrew Murdison and some of the other men enough courage to enter the hotel after him. They found Johnston in the kitchen, an open razor clutched in his hand attempting, it appeared, to cut his own throat. Murdison launched himself at Johnston and the two men fell grappling to the floor. The rest of the men rushed to help Murdison. Walter Dalgleish, the blacksmith, tried to wrest the razor from Johnston's grasp. So tightly did Johnston hold on to it that the brawny blacksmith had to use tongs to prise it from the struggling man's grasp. Eventually the combined weight of the men overcame Johnston. His arms and legs were bound with rope and he was carried upstairs and laid on a bed. Despite his trussed-up state he continued to thrash and throw himself about. Gradually he tired and with his exhaustion a certain calmness overtook him. He started to talk to his captors and told them that he had been going to the moors to shoot a hare and had been cleaning the gun when it went off accidentally. He then burst into a fit of weeping and sobbed, "I dearly lo'e my wife." It was a story he was to stick to despite all the evidence to the contrary.

Two hours later the local constable arrived and took Johnston into custody. When he was placed in a cell he was so agitated that it was thought wise to have him constantly supervised. He could not rest and paced up and down his cell, occasionally giving vent to loud outbursts of grief and protestations of how much he loved his wife. After being examined and charged, he was removed to Greenlaw prison where it was reported that he slept and ate well and that his state of mind was 'good'. That mood changed somewhat when, on the 8th April 1878 he appeared before the judge, Lord Craighill, at Jedburgh High Court on a charge of murder. The indictment read, "....In so far as upon the twelfth day of December eighteen seventy-seven, in a court or yard situated at the back of the Commercial Hotel, then occupied by himself and Euphemia Davidson or Waugh or Johnston, did discharge a gun loaded with powder and shot or leaden pellets at her person, part or all of which did strike her and did penetrate her head, face, and other parts of her person in consequence of which she immediately or soon after died." In a barely audible voice Johnston pleaded 'Not Guilty' and appeared somewhat morose and despondent to many of the observers in court.

Such was the intense interest aroused by the case that a great number of people were refused admittance to the courtroom which was crowded almost to bursting point. Johnston had been brought over to Jedburgh from Greenlaw the night before. A great number of people wanted to see him and all the streets and passages leading to the court house were packed. So great was the press of people that one man suffered a pair of broken ribs. A considerable number of women were present in the courtroom, intently following the proceedings. A commentator was to remark that the trial was more about the position or rights of women in society than punishing the prisoner.

Several witnesses who were called on his behalf were prepared to testify that his gun was very light on the trigger. In particular, Robert Swanston, a slater in Earlston recalled how Johnston's gun had gone off accidentally during a pigeon shooting contest. Johnston, continued to claim that the shooting of his wife was accidental. He said that at the breakfast table that morning his wife had suggested that he go to the moor and shoot some rabbits. He had gone outside to clean the gun and was in the middle of doing this when the guard had caught in a cloth that he had wrapped around a sore thumb. The gun had gone off and his wife had been struck in the head as she was walking across the yard with two pails of bran to feed the cows. He also claimed that his step-daughter, Grace, had tried to turn her mother against him.

It was, however, his step-daughter's evidence which was to prove decisive. She disclosed that Johnston had threatened to shoot her mother in October when they had quarrelled over the lease of the hotel. Andrew Murdison was to confirm that Mrs. Johnston had told him of her husband's threats though when he challenged Johnston about it, Johnston said that it had been a joke. Grace also said that there had been no mention of Johnston going out to shoot rabbits at the breakfast table that morning. Indeed most of the conversation had centred around his laziness. Mrs. Johnston had said to him during breakfast that, "If you would go and work and try and help me we would be better!" Johnston had listened but had not said very much. When Susan McGuire was called she was able to confirm most of Grace's evidence. After hearing the servant girl's evidence, Mr. Balfour, the counsel for the defence, announced that his client was withdrawing his original plea and would now plead 'Guilty' to the reduced charge of 'culpable homicide'. This was accepted by Lord Craighill who then told the jury that they would have to pass a verdict of 'guilty' to the charge of 'culpable homicide'. The jury concurred with this without leaving their seats. When passing sentence the judge said that "Culpable homicide is a charge of very wide comprehension. It ranges from that which is little more than a mere inception of a crime to that which comes to the very borders of murder. Your crime comes up to the verge of murder. I think there is no escape from that conclusion." He added that it was necessary to inflict a heavy punishment. John Johnston was sentenced to penal servitude for fifteen years. The judge added, "I hope that during your long interval of seclusion from the world you will think of the past, and do what you can to atone for your offence, so that when you return to the world you will be a very different man from the man you were when you were apprehended."

It was a verdict that did not meet with the approval of the local population. There was a widespread belief that it was a brutal and premeditated murder. To many it seemed like a miscarriage of justice. It may be, however, that the prosecution considered that it might have been difficult to prove a charge of murder beyond a reasonable doubt. Johnston may not have actually planned the murder in any great detail but his mood of the night before and on the morning of the murder suggests that he brooded much on his imagined grievances him and when the opportunity arose he was predisposed to kill. "Few will be able to see" wrote a local newspaper, "any difference between this case and many others for which sentence of death is passed."

John Johnston waxed highly indignant at the turn of events. He objected to his lawyer pleading guilty to the lesser charge of culpable homicide. In his opinion if his lawyer had not done this he reckoned he would have been found 'Not Guilty' or at the very least "Not Proven.' There was certainly little sign that he felt any sense of atonement as the judge had wished. He would have had a long time to ponder the verdict, however; a few days after the trial he was escorted by train to Perth prison to start his prison sentence.

John Johnston is still remembered in Earlston and it is claimed that he returned to the area after serving only 8 years of his sentence.

Getting There

The Commercial Hotel stood on the High Street in Earlston. It is now a private house situated next to the Post Office. The yard at the back where Mrs Johnston met her death has not greatly changed. Although the outbuildings serve different functions they are roughly in the same place as they were in 1878.

The Castle, Galashiels

Murder in the Castle

Galashiels November 1880

Gala folk had never really taken to the ugly, five storey tenement building referred to locally as 'The Castle'. It had been built in 1849 to house workers employed in the building of the railways which at that time was becoming the major growth industry in the Borders. Most of the workers were a rough and ready lot. Many were young, unmarried Irishmen who had developed the habit of getting very drunk on pay day and indulging in drunken brawls, most often among themselves, but sometimes with the local lads. The inhabitants of 'The Castle' did not stay for long; the nature of their work meant that when one piece of track had been laid, the workers moved on to the next place. Long after the period of railway construction was over the building continued to be regarded as a place of 'last resort'. It developed a reputation as a building where only the lowest sections of Galashiels society lived. Long after it had been demolished and its memory almost forgotten, old men would say that it was, "A howff o' right scunners and Irish ne'er dae weels". Certainly this was the view of Gala folk in 1880 when 'The Castle' was to acquire a darker stain on its already tarnished reputation.

In November 1880, David Keenan and Elizabeth Park lived in a two-roomed flat on the second floor of The Castle. He was Irish and had probably met Elizabeth in Liverpool. Elizabeth was a native of Galashiels though her father was, for a while, the innkeeper of the St

Ronan's Hotel in Innerleithen. When she was a young woman she had gone to Liverpool with a musician named Broadhurst. It is not clear if they had actually married but he died and she took up with Keenan. The pair came back to Galashiels and took up residence in The Castle in May 1878. In November 1880 both David Keenan and Elizabeth Park were in their early 50s. It would appear that their relationship was childless. It was not a happy partnership. Elizabeth was prone to bouts of heavy drinking and when drunk could be violently abusive towards Keenan. If he was sober he would usually ignore her tirades but if he had been drinking he would turn on her. Neighbours grew used to the sounds of their quarrels and most of them felt sympathy for David Keenan for they said that Elizabeth had "such a provoking tongue." This was despite the fact that on several occasions Elizabeth had fled into a neighbour's house followed by an enraged Keenan who proceeded to kick her with great violence. It was not surprising then that many of the neighbours had reckoned that this turbulent relationship would end in tragedy.

Extended drinking parties were not uncommon in the Keenan household and Saturday the 20th November 1880 was no exception. From early afternoon a steady stream of people came into the house where a fair measure of drinking combined with revelry and the occasional argument took place. Nothing out of the ordinary was the opinion of most witnesses. The party continued well into the evening with people constantly coming and going, usually going out to purchase more drink. Most of the witnesses were later to testify that Keenan, though the worse of drink, was not particularly drunk. Elizabeth, on the other hand, was described as being very drunk. By ten o'clock most of the company had departed and quiet descended on the household and on 'The Castle'. It was not to last.

About half past ten a neighbour heard Betsy cry "Murder!" but as she heard nothing else she thought little of it until the next day. Around the same time another neighbour heard Betsy cry "Oh!" As she also heard nothing else and later observed that no lights were showing in the Keenan's house, she concluded that they had gone to bed.

Around midnight the Keenan's neighbour, Elizabeth Mabon, who lived 'but and ben' from the Keenans, was woken by David Keenan coming into her house and asking her to "Come and see what's wrong with Betsy". Keenan was upset and crying and added that Betsy had fallen off the chair and that he couldn't get her to speak. Mrs Mabon rose and went into Keenan's house. The single room was dimly lit with a paraffin lamp and a fire that burned brightly in the grate. On one side of the fireplace was an armchair where Keenan usually sat, on the other was an ordinary chair and about two feet from it lay the prone body of Elizabeth Park. She lay on the floor lying on her left side with her knees drawn up towards her chin. By her head was a large pool of blood. Mrs Mabon bent down and touched Elizabeth's cheek. It was stone cold. She looked up at David Keenan and said, "This woman is dead". David Keenan had sat down in the armchair and refused to believe that she was dead claiming that she had only fallen off the chair. Mrs Mabon called in some neighbours. One of those who was called was Elizabeth's brother, Thomas Park, who also lived in 'The Castle'. In his testimony he said that he was confronted by a weeping Keenan who sobbed, "Take me away and hang me up at once." Park told him to be quiet or he would incriminate himself. The local doctor arrived and he confirmed that Elizabeth Park was indeed dead. A little after one o'clock a local policeman arrived. He noted the blood on the floor and on Elizabeth's forehead and listened to the inebriated Keenan's protestations that he had not killed her and that she had only fallen off the chair. The constable was sceptical of Keenan's story and proceeded to take him into custody where he was formally charged with the murder of Elizabeth Park.

The trial of 51 year old David Keenan took place at the Jedburgh Circuit Court on the 5th April 1881. On that morning the presiding Judge Lord Craighill had made his way from the Spread Eagle Hotel to the Court House. He was accompanied by the Lord Provost of Jedburgh and several magistrates as well as the brightly dressed town-heralds. A large number of spectators were in the streets to watch the procession. All the public seats in the Court were occupied with a large number of women present in the gallery. When the charge against David Keenan was read out and he was asked how he pled, he stated in a clear and firm voice that he was 'Not Guilty'.

The issue for both the prosecution and the defence was a fairly straightforward one. Did Elizabeth Park die as a result of the injuries she received from falling off a chair or did she die as a result of blows inflicted by David Keenan? David Brand, the Advocate General who led the prosecuting team, produced a series of witnesses who had been in Keegan's house during the fateful day, and neighbours who testified what they had seen and heard. Others were called to comment on the fiery relationship between David Keegan and Elizabeth Park. A number of potentially useful witnesses, however, did not appear because they could not remember anything of significance having been drunk at the time, others had left Galashiels during the five month period between November and May and could not be found.

Two doctors called by the prosecution stated quite firmly that the injuries on Elizabeth Park's forehead were much more severe than would have been expected from a simple fall from a chair. It was conceded however, that much of the blood around the victim may have come from a cut on her finger. A pair of tongs was produced but as David Keenan denied that they belonged to him, the prosecution could not make much headway in trying to show that it was the murder weapon. The defence team called no witnesses as they felt confident that the prosecution would be unable to disprove David Keenan's repeated assertion that he had not struck Elizabeth and that she had fallen off a chair.

When David Brand stood up to make his final submission to the jury, he conceded that there was not sufficient evidence to sustain a charge of murder but submitted that David Keenan was guilty of culpable homicide. In his summing-up he reminded the jury of the events of the fateful day. He described the party atmosphere that prevailed at the house and how both Keenan and Elizabeth had got drunk and had fallen out. He reminded them of Elizabeth's cry of 'Murder!' and showed how Keenan had lied when he said that he had gone for help immediately after she had fallen. The evidence of the witnesses had shown how he had been some time in the room after Elizabeth had been injured. He concluded by citing the medical evidence whereby two doctors had stated quite clearly that Elizabeth's injuries were too severe to have been caused by a simple fall from a chair.

Mr Baxter for the defence was brief. He pointed out that the prosecution had been unable to prove that David Keenan had struck his wife a fatal blow and that there were no bloodstains on his clothes. After being out for all of six minutes, it appeared that the jury agreed, if somewhat reluctantly, One of them voted for a 'guilty' verdict but the majority decision was 'not proven'. In effect, they were saying that while they agreed that there was insufficient evidence to convict Keenan; they had major reservations about his innocence. Such technicalities however, did not concern David Keenan too much as he walked from the court a free man.

Getting There

'The Castle' stood in what is now Magdala Terrace in Galashiels. Coming into Galashiels on the A7 from Edinburgh. About 500 yards on there is a railinged gap between buildings on the right hand side of the road. These are still referred to as 'The Castle railings'. the castle was a 5 storey building on the other side of these railings. Entry was by means of bridge over a retaining wall and a passageway. No doubt this reminded Gala folk of a moat and helped the building be referred to as 'The Castle.' No trace remains of it today as it was demolished -along with many of its memories - in 1907.

Coldsmouth Gate
With the dyke and the burn in the foreground

Death in the Hills

November 15th 1880 Cheviot Hills

It was late afternoon on November 15th 1880. Deep in the Cheviot Hills, John Taylor the shepherd at Heathpool was on the hillside. Down below he spotted two men. Now this was a fairly unusual occurrence in these isolated and sparsely populated hills. He decided to go down and see what they were up to. He was suspicious as he could see that they had dogs with them and they were hanging around the rabbit warren, which had recently been leased to Mr Rankine, giving him sole right to any rabbits in the warren. As he approached the men his suspicions were confirmed for, in addition to the two dogs, the men also had a ferret. Ferrets were used by poachers to either kill or frighten the rabbits out of their holes. He asked them what they were doing and one of them replied that they were taking "a bit rabbit." Taylor said that it was not right that they should be taking rabbits from a man that had paid for them. It was a point of view that did not impress the two poachers. They grunted and went on with their preparations. The shepherd asked them what they were "hawkin" with." One of the poachers said, "I'll knock your head off with it," and grabbed hold of the old man. The shepherd was not so easily beaten and pushed his assailant off and stood in front of the rabbit hole with his hands on his hips. One of the men approached Taylor and slowly and deliberately spat in his face.The shepherd realised that the situation was turning ugly and decided to leave. He hurried off with the intention of finding the the local policeman or Thomas Allan who was the estate gamekeeper.

It was a cold, clear, star-filled night with a full moon shining above as Police Constable Scott made his way from the police station at Shotton on the road to Kilham, the frost covered track crunching beneath his measured tread. Out of the darkness he saw Thomas Allan approaching. As he got nearer he could see that Allan was somewhat excited and agitated. The gamekeeper told him about the encounter between the poachers and John Taylor at Heathpool. From the descriptions that the shepherd had given it was obvious to the two men that the poachers were a pair of gypsies well-known to the policeman and the gamekeeper. Indeed, one of them, John Tait (locally known as 'Stovy Jock') had only recently come out of prison after being convicted of a violent assault on the same Thomas Allan. The other man was William Blyth. Both of them came from Kirk Yetholm just over the border in Scotland.

Both gamekeeper and policeman reckoned that the poachers would be making their way back to Kirk Yetholm from Heathpool. They decided that the best place to intercept them was at Coldsmouth gate. It was along a road with a dry-stane dyke on one side and a small burn or ditch in front of it, which marked the boundary between Scotland and England. The two men quickened their pace and soon arrived at Coldsmouth where they stood and awaited the arrival of the two gypsies.

They heard them before they saw them. The raised voices and laughter of the two poachers carried down the hill in the still night air. Tait and Blyth had no reason to feel wary and were pleased with their day's work. Each man had ten rabbits slung over his shoulder and a couple more in their voluminous pockets. The dogs ran beside them as they approached Coldsmouth gate. From there it was an easy walk to Kirk Yetholm and home where they no doubt anticipated a savoury meal of freshly caught rabbit. It was, therefore, with some consternation that they saw two familiar, if unwelcome, figures standing before the gate.

The constable strode forward. He stated that he had reason to believe that they had illegally acquired game in their possession and that they had assaulted John Taylor, shepherd at Heathpool. He said he wanted to search them. The shocked poachers took the rabbits off their shoulders and laid them on the road, making no resistance. When the constable searched them he extracted from their pockets a number of rabbits as well as their ferret. Let us hope he searched carefully for the latter. He then informed them that he was going to confiscate the rabbits.

This was too much for the two men. Tait cursed and swore at the policeman and shouted that he would die rather than give them up. He picked up the rabbits from the road and threw them over the dyke, effectively into Scotland. Blyth jumped over the dyke but Tait was restrained by Scott who grabbed hold of him. The gamekeeper went over the dyke after Blyth but made no attempt to seize hold of him. Tait shouted to Blyth, "Pick up a stone and fell the bugger!" Blyth took a large stone from the dyke and hurled it at the policeman. It struck him full on the head. He let go of Tait and started to fall but recovered and slowly got to his feet. Tait grabbed a large coping stone from the dyke and brought it crashing down on the head of the unfortunate policeman who collapsed into the small burn that marked the border at this spot. By now Scott was semi-conscious with his head under the water in the burn. Tait continued to savagely beat the policeman with a thick stick. By this time Thomas Allan had seized hold of Blyth. He jumped back over the dyke to where Scott was lying and lifted his head out of the water and laid it on the bank. Tait flourished his stick and said he would kill the pair of them. Allan's gun was loaded. He looked at Tait, "If you throw another stone or touch me with that stick, I will blow a hole right through you." Tait paused. He stared into the gamekeeper's eyes. Then he turned away and vaulted the dyke. He and Blyth picked up the rabbits and disappeared into the night towards Kirk Yetholm. Allan picked up the stricken policeman, who was convinced that he was going to die, and slowly and painfully they began to make their way to his home at Paston.

Police Constable Scott was not a particularly robust man. He had suffered a fractured skull and sustained severe bruising to his body.

However, he was able to make a detailed statement about the incident. As a result, the two men were quickly arrested. Blyth was picked up in Kirk Yetholm and Tait in Melrose, where he had fled hoping that he would not be noticed. Blyth was quite unashamed and when he was arrested he said, "I wish I had killed him, better to hang sooner than syne." He complained that everybody had it in for him and that he couldn't find work and that was why he had to go poaching. His words had a fateful resonance. A few days after their arrest Constable Scott developed lockjaw from his injuries and died painfully a few days later, leaving a wife and five children. Tait and Blythe were handed over to the North Northumberland police to await the outcome of the inquest.

Thomas Allan was the principal witness at the inquest into the death of Constable Scott. It was held at Paston police station and was a focus of intense interest in the rural community. The gamekeeper received a very rough ride from the Coroner. He thought it very strange that Allan should have put up with so much abuse from Tait whom he knew to be dangerous. In the coroner's view, Allan would have been within his rights to shoot him in the legs. He also made the point that the police officer had died carrying out a duty which should properly have been that of the gamekeeper. To complete the hapless gamekeeper's day, Tait stated that if Allan had seized hold of Blyth right away, "the stone would never have been thrown." In justification, Allan said that everything happened so quickly that he had no time to think properly. The jury, however, were unanimous in their opinion that the policeman had been 'wilfully murdered' by Tait and Blyth. The two men were taken to Wooler Police Station where they were formally charged with murder. From there, amidst great scenes of public excitement, they were transferred to Morpeth Jail to await trial.

The trial of John Tait and William Blyth took place at Northumberland Winter Assizes Crown court on the 13th January 1881. They were charged with, "...having feloniously, wilfully, and of malice aforethought, killed and murdered Thomas Henry Scott on the 15th November last." The jury was presented with the prosecution evidence from the shepherd, the gamekeeper and with medical practitioner. The defence made much of the fact that under English law, poacher's goods could only be confiscated by a policeman on the public highway. When Tait threw the rabbits over the dyke and Scott continued to insist that they be confiscated, he was, they claimed, operating illegally. Everything that followed was as a result of this illegal act committed by the policeman. Both men were found guilty of manslaughter. John Tait, who was described as dark, swarthy and sullen looking was sentenced to penal servitude for life. William Blyth appeared altogether much more cheerful, as he was sentenced to ten years. Indeed he even thanked the judge as he was led away to start his sentence.

There is an interesting footnote to this tale which I will leave to some other researcher to uncover. John Tait (or Stovie Jock) apparently managed to escape from his prison and made his way to the U.S.A. There he changed his name to Meyer or Mayer. We do not know if he prospered but apparently his descendants did. I do not know if any of them have come back and visited that lonely spot in the Cheviot hills where their ancestor committed such a violent crime .

Getting There

You make your way to Kirk Yetholm and then take the road to Shotton. You pass Yetholm Mains farm and shortly after crossing the border you will see a sign indicating a footpath on the right hand side of the road. If you walk along the footpath for a distance of one and a half miles you will come to Coldsmouth Gate. The burn and the dyke are still there and there is a gate but not. I suspect, the one that was in place on that fateful evening in November 1880.

North British Railway station, Peebles

Deadlier than the Male

Peebles 23rd March 1916.

Twenty-two year old Alexander Anderson was a sergeant in the Lanarkshire Yeomanry during the dark days of 1916 when the carnage of the first World War was at its most intense. However, Alexander was fortunate. He had been given an extended leave to carry out some duties in his capacity as the county road surveyor for Peeblesshire. He was thus able to stay at the family home on the outskirts of Peebles along with his widowed mother and three younger brothers. On the morning of the 23rd of March, he left as usual just before nine o'clock to go to his office. Two of his brothers left at the same time to go to school but his youngest brother, Thomas, remained at home as he was recovering from a bout of measles. Watching their departure were their mother, Elizabeth Anderson and Matilda Bryant, their 15 year old servant who had been working for Mrs Anderson for six weeks. Mrs Anderson had felt sorry for the girl who had been destitute and desperate for some kind of employment. At first she had worked well but Mrs Anderson had grown concerned about her as the weeks passed. The quality of her work had deteriorated and she was exhibiting, in Mrs Anderson's view, slovenly and dirty habits. Of even greater concern was the fact that several household ornaments and items of clothing had gone missing. Alexander knew of his mother's concern and was aware that she intended to report the matter to the police that morning. He also knew that she could not make up her mind about whether she should confront the girl before she saw the police.

Alexander was thus mildly surprised when he returned home at lunchtime and Matilda told him that his mother had gone off to Glasgow and would not be back in time for lunch. Apparently she had received a telegram from her sister saying that a relative there was unwell. The girl also told him that Mrs Anderson had intended to call at the home of Sir Henry Ballantyne at nearby Minden where Mrs Anderson's sister had stayed for a while. The girl then served lunch to Alexander and his brothers, without anything in her manner suggesting to him that anything out of the ordinary had occurred. Matilda apologised for the pudding not being quite ready and offered to make him a cup of tea instead. Lunch completed, Alexander returned to his work and his brothers went back to school. Nine year old Thomas remained in the house. He had been playing in the garden for most of the morning and had made occasional forays into the kitchen where Matilda was working. She had laughed and joked with him as she made the lunch. He had not seen his mother leaving. About three o'clock the maidservant told Thomas, who had gone back out into the garden, that she was going to catch a train at the North British station and asked him if he wanted to see her off. She told him to run ahead of her. When he arrived at the station the train was at the platform. It left without him seeing Matilda. Young Thomas shrugged and headed back home, meeting on the way his two brothers who were returning home from school.

That afternoon several people on the platform of the Caledonian station, noticed a young girl wearing a long black fur coat and expensive fur mittens. She got into conversation with Bessie Cunningham, a station porter's wife. The girl told Bessie that she had been on holiday in Peebles and thought she might return to stay at the local Hydro. She seemed a bit annoyed when she was told that she would have to wait until half past four before the next train for Glasgow. She chatted with Bessie for some time. In the course of the conversation she told Bessie that her name was Scougall and that her father and two uncles had been killed in the war and that her father had been awarded a posthumous Victoria Cross. She also said she had a brother at the front and a sister who was a nurse in Belgium who had received an award for bravery. Both Bessie and her husband, who had joined them, said that she had a very natural manner and spoke very politely without a 'Scotch' accent. John Cunningham said she behaved as if she was a lady's daughter but both he and his wife noticed that she had 'servant's hands'. They both thought her a little strange, and that despite her expensive airs, she was probably a servant going to a new position. As the Glasgow train pulled out of the station the girl smiled and waved to the porter and his wife.

At about quarter to five Alexander Anderson was just tidying up his office desk before finishing for the day. His door suddenly burst open and his excited young brothers rushed into his office to say that the house was a mess and that the maid had gone. He hurried home. After unlocking the door he found pots and pans lying on the kitchen floor and the lunch dishes still on the table. He went upstairs to the bedrooms and found drawers pulled out and his mother's jewel case lying on the bed of the spare room. Some clothing was scattered about. Alexander immediately concluded that they had been burgled. As he passed the open door of the servant's room, which lay just off the kitchen, he noticed a bundle of bedclothes lying on the floor. He paid it little attention and hurried out to inform the police of the robbery. A neighbour took care of his brothers while Alexander set off for Minden to see if his mother was there. They had not seen her and knew nothing of her sister's illness. Alexander then went to the Post Office where he learned that no telegrams had been sent to his home. By now Alexander was thoroughly concerned and he headed back home. He got back and started to tidy up the house. When he entered the maidservant's room, he tried to pick up the pile of bedclothes next to the bed. There was something heavy underneath. Uncovering it he discovered the body of his mother. Her head was lying in a pool of blood and despite his horror and distress he could not help noticing that she still had her hat on as if she had been intending to go out.

There were no signs of a struggle but Mrs Anderson had died as a result of repeated blows on the head from an axe which was later found in a coal bunker. It was quickly established that the girl calling herself

Matilda Bryant had caught the four thirty train to Glasgow and that she had been wearing clothing stolen from the dead woman. A telegram was sent to the Glasgow police to intercept the girl but they were too late as the train had already arrived in Glasgow. In the course of their enquiries the police also learned that the girl's name was not Matilda Bryant, she was Jeanne Larsson and she had absconded from a girl's detention centre in Loanhead, just outside Edinburgh, some two months before. The girl had been convicted in Aberdeen for theft and had been sent to the detention centre until she was nineteen. Jeanne Larsson was only fifteen and had got the name of Matilda Bryant from a character in a sketch that she and the other girls in the centre had taken part in at Christmas.

The police were concerned that the girl would vanish without trace among the teeming population of the City of Glasgow; she had not been seen since she had boarded the train on Thursday afternoon. The police did have some leads however. The girl had told Mrs Anderson where her relatives in Glasgow stayed and the Peeblesshire constabulary immediately contacted their counterparts in Glasgow. Chief Detective Inspector McKay of the St Rollox Division was put in charge of the search for the girl. At first the search for Jeanne proved fruitless. On the Saturday morning Inspector McKay learned that two girls, one of whom fitted Jeanne's description, had stayed at a YWCA building in Bath Street on the Thursday night but had left in the morning without leaving a forwarding address. A link was made with a Girls' Home in Bridgeton. The police visited the home on Sunday morning but were told that Jeanne had gone to church. The police waited outside the Mission Hall she was attending and followed her as she entered a confectionery shop in Main Street. They found her sitting in the back room of the shop with another girl. Inspector McKay looked at Jeanne and said, "Lift up your furs and come with me".

The girl with Jeanne was Lizzie Whyte, who worked in the shop and was stunned when the police burst in to arrest the young girl she had met only the night before. She said that Jeanne had come into her shop in the early evening of the day before. Lizzie had commented on the lovely fur and muff she was wearing and Jeanne said she had got it as a present from her 'mamma'. Lizzie noticed that the girl was shivering, despite her furs, and invited her into the back room of the shop to heat herself at the stove. The two girls got chatting. Jeanne said that her name was Hilda Smith and that she was only in Glasgow for a holiday. She showed Lizzie a ring with a green stone which she said had been given to her by a soldier who was now at the front. Lizzie noticed how talkative the girl was and that she tended 'to put on airs' and that sometimes her speech was 'rather Anglified' but that she occasionally gave herself away by lapsing into her native accent. The observant Lizzie also noticed that in contrast to the expensive furs, the rest of 'Hilda's' clothes were of poor quality. In spite of this Lizzie was totally charmed by the girl who said she found it rather lonely in the big city. Lizzie immediately suggested that they go to the pictures together on the Thursday night when she had some time off, adding that it would cost about twopence or threepence. 'Hilda' agreed but spoilt the offer by saying that a shilling was more her style. She confided in Lizzie that she had been out with an army officer the previous night and had gone with him to a restaurant in Argyle Street where she drank port and smoked ladies' cigarettes. The officer had given her his card but she would have to hide it from her 'mamma' as she would be most upset. She stayed chatting to Lizzie in the shop for about an hour during which time she managed to tell her that her sister was a nurse at the front who had been decorated for devotion to duty and that another sister was engaged to an army captain. She added wistfully that she would like to be a nurse but in another year she would qualify as a schoolteacher. When she left, Lizzie had the distinct impression that she was going to meet her officer friend of the previous evening.

Jeanne had actually spent the Saturday night at the Home for Girls in Bridgeton where she had impressed the matron as being "a very nice, quiet girl". When the police entered Lizzie Whyte's shop that Sunday morning, Lizzie noticed that Jeanne's face flared up as red as fire. She seemed to be more embarrassed about being caught out lying to Lizzie than she was upset about being arrested for murder. Jeanne remained cool and unperturbed during her arrest. When the charges were read out to her her manner was so detached that Chief Inspector McKay was not sure that she recognised the serious nature of her position. When formally charged with murder she said, "I never murdered her! I took the furs but I never murdered her!"

Jeanne Larsson presented a problem for the Children's Court in Glasgow; no child had ever been charged with murder in its history. It was also hard for the magistrates to believe that the young girl of quiet and demure appearance, who stood before them, could have committed such a dreadful crime. She was not charged with murder as she was still, in the eyes of the law, a child; instead she was charged with culpable homicide, in that "she assaulted Elizabeth Jane Fergusson or Anderson of Bonnington Road, Peebles, beat her on the head with an axe and killed her." She was then transferred into the hands of an Inspector Hodge and a female officer who accompaned the girl back to Peebles Sheriff Court. From there she would be committed to the Calton prison in Edinburgh. By this time word had spread around Peebles that the girl had been brought back. Feelings about the killing were running high, for the Fergusson family were held in high regard by the local people. The police were concerned for the safety of Jeanne and it was decided that she should board the Edinburgh train at the small village of Eddlestone about four miles from Peebles. No one there took much notice of the policeman, who was in civilian clothes and the lady who walked arm in arm with a pale, young looking girl dressed in a smart, navy blue costume. The next day Peebles town bell tolled mournfully as the funeral cortege wound its way through the town to the cemetery where Mrs Anderson was buried surrounded by large numbers of mourners - the victim of her own kindness.

Jeanne Larsson plead guilty at the High Court in Edinburgh to the charge of 'culpable homicide' with all the nonchalance that had marked her behaviour after the murder and when she was arrested. Mr Gilchrist, her defence lawyer, said that the circumstances surrounding the case were extraordinary in as much as there appeared to be no motive for the crime. The girl had been examined by doctors, including Dr Robertson, superintendent of Morningside Asylum. He said it was clear that the girl was lacking in 'mental balance'. "From the age of six..." he declared, "she has shown extraordinary perversity and has not developed morally." The Solicitor General remarked that "only statute prevented the inflicting of the ordinary punishment for such a crime. The accused had had an unfortunate history. She was a person of incorrigible criminality and a danger to society."

Lord Justice Clerk sentenced her to ten years detention adding that only the Secretary of State had the authority to shorten this period and he would only do so if he felt there were signs that she had reformed and did not any longer constitute a danger to society.

So who was Jeanne Larsson? This girl who was labelled an 'incorrigible criminal' from the age of six and who was to commit a dreadful murder before she was sixteen. Jeanne was born in Aberdeen in 1901, the daughter of a local girl and a Swedish sailor who died of influenza in Aberdeen when Jeanne was five years old. His widow was left in rather straitened circumstances, having to bring up Jeanne and her two sisters. There was a suggestion that the girls were neglected while Mrs Larsson, with the support of friends, trained to become a maternity nurse. If this was the case, there is no record of the elder sisters getting into any trouble; it was Jeanne who was to become the problem - almost from the time her father died.

Jeanne's criminal record dated from when she started primary school. Her headmaster was to write that she was addicted to pilfering and lying from an early age. She had also, apparently, made a false accusation against a teacher,the nature of which is not known, but which caused a great deal of distress. When she was seven years old she was expelled from a children's party in her local church because of her disruptive behaviour. The minister took her outside to remonstrate with her and was under the impression that he had successfully appealed to the better side of her nature. Her reaction to his pleas, however, was to head straight back into the church where she switched off the gas main and plunged the whole place into darkness. It was an incident that still rankled in the mind of the minister when he wrote describing it to the Solicitor General nine years later. He had no doubt of the total lack of morals of the young Jeanne. He was able to link up her lying and stealing with what he referred to as 'sexual depravity', for he also wrote that at the age of eight she was found in the room of "a labouring man who was suspected of using lewd behaviour towards her." When she was questioned she confessed to having been there before and that "she was aware of the man's object in asking her to the room." A classic case of the victim being labelled as the criminal.

Jeanne's career of thieving continued; no amount of punishments, threats, exhortations or police warnings seemed to have any effect on her. Her mother had lost control of her and so too did several girls' training institutions to which she was sent. She was removed from them because of her "bad influence" on the other girls. At the age of 12 she was boarded out in the country but her guardians refused to keep her as she stole money from them. It would appear that at this time Jeanne's mother disowned her, for she went off to Glasgow leaving Jeanne in the care of an aunt in Aberdeen who also found Jeanne more than she could handle. At the age of 14 she was in the Stonehaven Poorhouse when she was charged with fraud. Apparently she had pretended to be collecting money for a church fund. What made it extraordinary was that a month previously she had been picked up by the police for committing exactly the same offence in the same place! It was almost as if she wanted to be caught. That same year she was sent to the Dalry Reformatory in Loanhead from which she was to abscond and make her way to Peebles.

The authorities had a problem with Jeanne Larsson after she had been sentenced to ten years' detention. What on earth were they going to do with her? She was still technically a child and prison might prove totally unsuitable. Her defence solicitor had found the crime so extraordinary that he had called for a report on her mental condition. She was examined at length by two prominent doctors who declared that, "she displayed evil tendencies of a pronounced and incorrigible nature from an early age, and we are clearly of the opinion that her moral self is defective and has not developed as it does in every normal person. She also suffers from weakness of the power of self-control where her own selfish interests and impulses are involved and is not deterred from wrongdoing by the consequences of her own actions." They also pointed out that she did not appear to realise the dreadful nature of her crime nor appreciate the seriousness of her situation. She showed no feelings of remorse and tended to blame other people. Their conclusion was that Jeanne was a lunatic, "that is to say", they went on, " ... a person so affected in mind by reasons of defect of the moral sense and weakness of the power of self-control, as to be rendered unfit, in our opinion, to be at large as regards the safety of the persons and property of others." She was however, they said, capable of pleading to the indictment. The authorities had several options; she could be placed in an asylum, possibly for the criminally insane, she could be placed in an adult prison or she could be placed in a juvenile centre. There were problems with all these options but it was finally decided that she should be placed in the Borstal Institution of Duke Street Prison in Glasgow under close supervision with regular reports on her to be sent to the Scottish Office.

Early reports from the prison governor suggest that the trauma of the trial had had very little effect on Jeanne. It was stated that she had tried to incite some of the other inmates to insubordination and that when the governor herself had reprimanded her, "her whole expression changed, and her face exhibited a mental conflict which was painful to witness." A little later the report is more positive. Her conduct had been good, inasmuch as she had not infringed any of the rules and had been fairly industrious. She did better at work calling for manual effort than that which required "slight mental concentration." She was fond of reading and spent a lot of her spare time with books, "though mostly light and sensational fiction." She also liked to draw and apparently displayed some skill in this. On the negative side the report went on to state that she was very vain and proud of her personal appearance and that she displayed "none of the naturalness looked for in a girl of her years." She expressed no regret for her crime but was not lacking in intelligence and was always looking for sympathy and admiration. She concluded her report by saying, "I regard her like a strong animal confined in a fragile cage which some day, sooner or later, her virile strength will snap the bars asunder." She was convinced that confinement would do no good for the girl and that outside field work with strong supervision would be the ideal treatment for her.

Jeanne herself petitioned the Scottish Secretary to reconsider the terms of her confinement. The language is mature and the writing confident. In this petition she states that: "The past is black, the present intolerable and the future is almost as black as the past." In July 1918 an interview was arranged between Jeanne and her estranged mother. This seemed to lift her spirits somewhat, though her mother did not respond to her letters for some time. In 1920 she was transferred to the Jessiefield Institution in Dumfries but this was not a success. Jeanne was unhappy and again petitioned the Secretary of State, this time to be allowed to return to Glasgow: " I have tried and am sorry to say, have failed. I dare say I am at fault; but I can't forget that I am spending the best years of my life in prison and that these years are all but wasted ones (or so it seems to me). Even mother has stopped writing." She was now two months short of her twentieth birthday.

On the 9th of November 1920 it was recommended that Jeanne Larsson be liberated under licence to the care of the Salvation Army in London as they had indicated a willingness to look after her. Jeanne headed south in January of the following year. It was not a success, however. In August the Scottish authorities received a terse telegram from Adelaide Cox of the Salvation Army :- " Regret inform you Miss Larsson - mind abnormal. Kindly remove from here." An escort was sent and Jeanne Larsson was taken back to prison in Edinburgh and the licence revoked. It had obviously not been a good experience for her. She was reported by the medical staff to be conceited and unstable and "her lack of moral sense and self-control render her a potential danger to others." One of the doctors delivered an even more damning report in which he wrote:- "Her self-conceit has grown greatly. She has received too much praise for what she can do and has had her attention too little directed to the things she cannot do well. She has made no improvement in her ability to earn a living or to look after herself. She is still a potential danger to others if offended."

In January of 1922 the Salvation Army were once again prepared to take in Jeanne, who was now aged 21 and applied for her conditional liberation. The prison staff still regarded her as 'undependable' and it was not until the following December that she was released into the Army's care and placed in their home in Pollokshields in Glasgow. In 1924 she was transferred to an Army home in Manchester where, while there was no suggestion that she was not doing well, it was felt that a change of environment would be good for her. In May 1927, over 10 years after her trial, Jeanne Larsson was handed over to the private guardianship of Mrs Jeannie Henderson in Fife. A note in the files states that Jeanne's mother had asked she travel by way of Glasgow in order that she could meet her and take her daughter to Fife.

From this point on the official records on Jeanne Larsson cease and no further mention is made of her. A search of the Marriage and Death Records in Scotland proved fruitless. It would appear that Jeanne did not stay long with Mrs Henderson and that she returned to England. Whether that was to another institution or if she managed to make a life for herself in society we cannot tell.

Postscript

Some time after writing this I received a newspaper cutting from a friend who knew that I was researching this murder. It was from the Daily Record for January 1929. In it was a report from the Berkshire Assizes in Reading. Jeanne, who was described as Jean Dawson (25) and who worked as a companion, was sentenced to eighteen months imprisonment for stealing £300 of jewellery from her employer. Mr Justice Roche said, " What you need is a lengthy term of reflection. Your one chance in life is to put your dishonesty behind you." It transpires that Jeanne had been sent to Canada, probably in the hope that she could start a new life. It did not work out; for she was deported from that country after having being found guilty of theft. It does not look as if there was any happy ending for Jeanne Larsson so it might be wise to draw a veil over her subsequent life.

A quiet street in Ednam

The Ednam Tragedy

8th December 1923 Ednam

The village of Ednam stands on the river Eden about two miles north-east of Kelso. It is possible that it is the river from which the name is derived - "the hamlet on the river Eden." Despite it being one of the earliest recorded settlements in the Borders, little of historical note has been handed down to us about Ednam. It was however, the birthplace of James Thomson, author of the once popular poem, 'The Seasons.' Although he is probably better remembered as the author of 'Rule Brittania' which was to become the anthem of the British Empire. Henry Francis Lyte was also born in Ednam. He was the man who wrote the popular hymn, 'Abide with Me.' A further footnote in the pages of history is the fact that the father of the famous explorer Captain Cook was born in the parish; his grandfather was an elder and member of the kirk session. If Ednam was not a name that loomed large in Scottish history then that was to change in 1923, when the village was rudely and dramatically flung into the full glare of the spotlight of national publicity as a result of what became known as 'The Ednam Tragedy.'

In 1923 the village had a population of less than two hundred people. Most were involved in agricultural work as their forebears had been for centuries. Many of the younger people however, were increasingly seeking employment in the burghs and the big cities. One of the people in the village in 1923 was sixty-two year old James Green who worked for the local blacksmith. He lived in a small house, not untypical of the accommodation for working -class people at that time. It consisted of a small entrance lobby; a kitchen, which was the main living quarters, with a smaller scullery kitchen just off it. Above this was a larger room or garret which was reached by a step-ladder in the kitchen and through a trap-door. James Green was a powerfully built man in good physical health. He was a widower but his son's wife lived in the house with her two children. She described herself as 'auld Jimmy's housekeeper'.

It was an arrangement which the villagers found extremely curious. On the 4th of July 1919, James Green's son, Robert, had married Margaret Annie Hogg of Kelso. They had been 'walking out' for five years before that, when Robert worked as an assistant in a bookshop in Kelso. On the outbreak of war in 1914 Robert signed up and served for the duration in the Royal Army Medical Corps. When the war ended Robert Green decided to sign on as a regular in the army. He came home and married Annie Hogg. They moved into his father's house, sharing the bed in the kitchen. After six days leave he returned to Aldershot. In November he was back for ten days sick leave and again for six days at Christmas. He was shortly afterwards to leave for Mesopotamia. He was not to return for another three years. In August 1920 Annie Hogg gave birth to a son - and in September 1921 she gave birth to another son.

When Mrs Green went to register the birth of the second child at the local Registrar's office she was, of course, asked the name of the father of the child. Her reply was 'auld Jimmy.' The Registrar was so disturbed that he informed the Lord Advocate's office in Edinburgh. They instructed the local Procurator Fiscal, Sydney Hilson to investigate. He interviewed Annie Green in his office in Jedburgh. Annie Green told him that after her husband had left for Mesopotamia, she and her child remained in his father's house, where she acted as the old man's housekeeper. She slept in a bed in the kitchen while he slept in the upstairs room. She said that on Saturday nights James Green usually went out drinking. He had a considerable reputation as a heavy drinker. One Saturday,towards the end of January 1921, she waited up for him as usual. He returned fairly late and in a drunken state. She served him his supper and, when he had finished his meal, she indicated that she wanted to retire to bed, expecting that her father-in-law would make his way up to his own bed. Instead, she claimed, he came over by the fire where she was sitting and started to 'canoodle' with her. She struggled to get away but he lifted her out of the chair and "had forcible connection with her." After about fifteen minutes he went upstairs to his room. It was, she stated, the only time it had happened. In his notes, Mr Hilson remarked, "The girl appeared to be somewhat simple and one who might easily be taken advantage of." If Annie Green was to be believed then she had been raped by her own father-in-law. There is no evidence that James Green was interviewed by the Fiscal but he was certainly informed that criminal proceedings could be taken against him if Annie Green continued to live with him. Annie Green did leave and went to her mother's house in Kelso but within a few weeks she was back living with the old man in Ednam.

In July 1922 Robert Green returned from Mesopotamia. He confronted his wife and father and they admitted that James Green was the father of Annie's second child. Robert Green was distraught, but remarkably he was determined to try and save his marriage. Several of his friends were to state that he seemed to be more upset by the behaviour of his father than by that of his wife. In March of 1923 Robert obtained an honourable discharge from the army. He managed to get a job at a hairdressers in Edinburgh and Annie agreed to move there with him together with the two children. According to Annie, Robert had promised that he would rent furnished rooms in Edinburgh. Instead, she found that they were lodging in a single room at the home of Robert's sister, Mrs Tice.

It was not a happy arrangement. Mrs Tice was to claim that Annie hardly ever spoke to her and was constantly talking to the children about 'old Jimmy' and Ednam. After a week Annie announced that she was leaving and was going back to live with her mother in Kelso. Robert was upset but saw his wife and the children off on the train. He said that he would look for work in England and that they would start a new life there. Annie went home to her mother's house but within two weeks had moved back again to Ednam and James Green's house. Robert continued to send his wife six shillings a week for the upkeep of his child. He wrote frequently to her but his bitterness spilt out when he told her to get ready to go to England with him, "There is only one child going with you. You can please yourself as to the other." Annie refused to leave the house in Ednam despite the protests of her husband and the pleas of her mother. "She was," said Mrs Tice, "perfectly obsessed with the old man."

On Friday the 8th of December 1923 Robert Green told his sister that he was going to visit a friend, John Haddow, who lived in Berryhill just outside Kelso. He arranged with his employer to have the Monday morning off. He carried no luggage with him other than his shaving razor, claiming he was very fussy about only shaving with his own razor. The Friday evening was spent at the home of Mrs Tice, his sister's mother-in-law. He left there at eleven o'clock saying that he was going to Berryhill. According to Mrs Tice, no mention was made of the situation in Ednam.

In his subsequent statement, Robert Green said that he set off intending to go to Berryhill but, as it was a fine, clear night he decided to go to Ednam instead. He had, he said, assumed that his father would be out and that he would try and persuade his wife to leave the house. He arrived in Ednam about quarter past eleven. He knocked at the door but got no answer. He rapped at the window. He heard his wife coming down the ladder and calling out, "Who is there?" He replied , "It's Rob." He then heard her call out that it was Rob and what should she do. After a while his father flung open the door and demanded to know what he was doing there. What happened next is, to a great extent, based on the words of Robert Green.

Robert was to claim that, after his father had asked him if he was looking for trouble, the old man had launched himself at him. He was seized by the throat and his father pressed his thumbs against his son's windpipe. Robert punched him in the face, in an attempt to dislodge him, but to no avail. Hanging on the wall in the vestibule was a German canister bomb that Robert had brought back from the war. Seizing it by its wooden handle, he struck his father a blow on the head. The father staggered back, clutching his bleeding head, and told Annie to go to a neighbour and fetch help. Annie fled from the house as the old man slumped down on to the sofa. Thinking the fight was over Robert put his hand in his pocket for some cigarettes. He took his razor out and used the handkerchief that it was wrapped in to wipe his face. Suddenly his father leapt up and attacked him again. He fended his father off with some punches but claimed that he had forgotten he had the razor in his hand. His father fell on to the sofa and then got up and went outside. He was, he said, quite unaware that his father was seriously injured.

Annie had meanwhile rushed across to the house of James Thomson who lived opposite. James Thomson was in bed, he got up and was told by a hysterical Annie that Robert was 'mauling' his father. He told her to go and fetch another neighbour and that he would follow. As he passed the Green's house he could see the outline of someone who appeared to be shadow boxing. He went to the neighbour's and told Annie to go to tell William Patterson at the Post Office. Annie came back and said that someone was lying in the gutter outside the Green's house. James Thomson went over and lit a match. It was James Green, dressed in his drawers and a shirt, his face congealed in blood. It was obvious to James Thomson that he was breathing his last. Meanwhile, Annie had been taken into the Paterson's house. William Paterson set off to Kelso to fetch a doctor and the police. Shortly after he left there was a knocking at the door. It was Robert Green. He asked Mrs Paterson to let him in. His father had punched him and he did not know where he had gone or where his wife was. Both women were petrified. Mrs Paterson said that William had locked the door and gone off with the key so she could not let him in. After a few moments Robert Green left. He went back to his father's house and lay down on the hearth rug, using his overcoat as a pillow. He was still there when the doctor arrived along with the police. He was, said the doctor, exhausted and in a state of nervous tension. The police took him away into custody. He made no resistance.

The trial of Robert Green for the murder of his father took place in a packed High Court in Jedburgh. He entered a plea of 'not guilty' and the court was told that a special plea of self-defence would be lodged. The defence made much of Robert Green's good character. His discharge papers stated that he was, "a hard-working, reliable and trustworthy man." Nobody could be found who would say a word against him. The fact that he had tried to effect a reconciliation with his wife was stressed despite the dreadful behaviour displayed by her and his father. The defence also claimed that Robert Green had only gone to Ednam to see his wife. The killing of his father was not intentional and was the result of a desperate attempt to ward of the attack of a stronger man. They claimed that, "far from showing a spirit of revenge the accused had shown a spirit of forbearance which was as much above the compass of ordinary human nature as murderous intent was below it".

The prosecution did not see it quite like that. The expert testimony of medical witnesses stated that the wounds suffered by James Green could not have been inflicted by accident. His friend, John Haddow, was quite unaware that Robert intended to visit him. They pointed out that the plea of self-defence rested only on the words of Robert Green. They also reminded the jury that merely because James Green was an immoral man, it did not make him a violent one.

During the course of the trial, Lord Constable pointed out that there was a case reported in 1731, where by a decision of the Court of Justiciary it was held that where a man discovered his wife in an act of impropriety with another man, the killing of that man was not murder. "You get very near that case here, where you get two people coming down from the same room undressed." Perhaps he had read the report by the policeman who had inspected the scene of the crime. Among the objects he had found in the upstairs room was a pair of lady's blue knickers. In her statement Annie Green admitted that the knickers were hers and that they had been " taken off her person by the deceased for the purpose of having connection with her just as the accused had knocked at the door."

In his lengthy charge to the jury before they retired to consider their verdict, he said that "certain painful features make this a difficult case for the jury. There was no doubt that Robert Green had inflicted the fatal wound. But his father had committed against him one of the most profound wrongs that one man could do to another. It would be difficult for the jury to hold the scales of justice equally."

In the event, the jury did not find it all that difficult. They were out for fifteen minutes and came back with a unanimous verdict of guilty of culpable homicide but with a strong recommendation for leniency. In passing sentence Lord Constable said that he was taking into account Robert Green's previously good character and the jury's plea. Robert Green was sentenced to eighteen months imprisonment. The verdict was greeted with great applause by the packed court room.

Robert Green divorced his wife in December 1924 while he was a prisoner in Saughton in Edinburgh and she was living with her mother in Kelso. Walter Green, the son of Annie Hogg and her father-in -law was lost at sea on the HMS Cossack in 1941. Robert Green served his sentence and remarried. He died at Bonnyrigg in 1956 . On his death certificate he is described as a carpet factory worker.

Getting There

If you take the B6461 from Kelso you reach the village of Ednam after two miles. On the right hand side is the old blacksmith's workshop where James Green probably worked. If you turn left you are on a street made up mainly of single storied terraced houses. It is a much more prosperous and comfortable looking place than it would have been in 1923. The street would have been unpaved and unlit with deep gutters, in one of which James Green was to breathe his last. His house has changed dramatically, being a substantial two storey building. Although the present occupants are well aware of the house's past history, it has not deterred them from turning it into a happy family home.

Index